The Chartered Institute of Management Accountants

CIMA

The Co-ordination of Mission Statements, Objectives and Targets in UK Executive Agencies

Noel Hyndman
University of Ulster at Jordanstown
Ron Eden
University of Ottawa, Canada

This publication arises from the research project 'An Empirical Study of the Co-ordination of Goals, Objectives and Targets in Executive Agencies' which was funded with a research grant from the CIMA Research Foundation. The award of a Research Foundation grant, and the publication of findings in this format, indicates that the recipient has successfully passed two separate peer review processes, which also involved practitioner assessors. The views expressed in this publication are the authors' own, and do not necessarily represent those of CIMA.

Acknowledgements

The authors wish to express their gratitude to all the UK executive agencies that provided both the annual reports and the business and corporate plans that formed the basis of the empirical studies in this report, and particularly to thank the chief executives who gave of their time to participate in the interviews. Finally, we should also like to thank the Chartered Institute of Management Accountants for the financial and research support of this project, and three anonymous referees for their very helpful comments.

First published in 2001 by:
The Chartered Institute of Management Accountants
63 Portland Place
London
W1B 1AB

ISBN 1 85971 464 1

Contents

About the Authors

Noel Hyndman is Professor of Management Accounting at the University of Ulster, having previously worked at the Queen's University of Belfast and the University of Ottawa in Canada. A fellow of the Chartered Institute of Management Accountants, he was awarded a PhD by the Queen's University of Belfast for his research in accounting for not-for-profit organisations. He has published widely in the area of public-sector and not-for-profit accounting, and has provided related consultancy support and training for a range of public-sector bodies.

Ron Eden is Assistant Professor at the University of Ottawa. A member of the Society of Management Accountants of Canada, he holds a PhD from the State University of New York for his work in the accounting and financing of local government. He has published in the area of public-sector accounting and has a particular interest in healthcare accounting.

Abbreviations

AAA	American Accounting Association
ASC	Accounting Standards Committee
DFP	Department of Finance and Personnel
FASB	Financial Accounting Standards Board
GASB	Government Accounting Standards Board
ICAS	Institute of Chartered Accountants of Scotland
NFPO	Not-for-profit organisation
NICS	Northern Ireland civil service
NPM	New Public Management
NPPI	Non-profit performance indicator
NSI	Next Steps Initiative

Executive Summary

This summary outlines the major themes in this research report. It provides a background to the emergence of executive agencies (agencies) and the increased focus on rational management ideas. It also presents the objectives of the empirical studies, together with the key findings.

The agency sector and rational management

The need to plan and control the performance of public-sector organisations with a view to improving performance has been a central issue in a number of UK government initiatives since 1979. A report by the Efficiency Unit (1988) to the Prime Minister argued that the civil service was too large and diverse to manage as a single unit, and that there was a need for smaller, performance-focused units. An extensive programme commenced, known as the Next Steps Initiative (NSI), aimed at delivering better-quality central-government services for the benefit of taxpayers, customers and staff. Agencies were established to carry out specific activities. By December 1998 138 agencies (113 in Britain and 25 in Northern Ireland) had been established, with 50 other units of government operating on Next Steps lines. In total, over 377,000 civil servants (76 per cent of all civil servants) were working in such organisations. Furthermore, another 19 candidates for agency status had been announced.

The NSI, as part of the wider New Public Management (NPM) movement[1], increased the emphasis on quantification in the public sector, specifically in the context of a highly rational model of management behaviour. Significant themes connected with rational management are that strategy should come about by highly systematised forms of planning, and that there is a need for specific and quantified targets. Ideas from the rational management literature, similar to those found in the writings of Drucker and Argenti, proliferate in many of the UK government publications related to planning and control in the public sector. An increased focus on targeting, measuring and reporting performance was promulgated. It was argued that performance information was necessary both to improve management within the public sector and to discharge accountability by the public sector.

In such a scheme, the importance of establishing clear links between the various levels of planning and control is often stressed. By having targets (that is, quantified, time-bound objectives) for performance and by measuring achievements against targets, a basis for better management within the public sector is provided. It is argued that this will give direction to activities and provide a basis for evaluating whether the organisation has been effective and efficient. Furthermore, such targets can provide a platform for the discharge of accountability. To facilitate such ideas within the agency sector, each organisation is required to produce a corporate plan, typically covering a three- to five-year period, with annual business plans being developed from this base. Performance targets, financial projections, assessments of prospects and other information are included in the plans. In addition, agencies are required to produce an annual report and accounts for each year of operation, which provide information on issues such as the agency's financial performance and its achievements against key targets. The annual report is available to all stakeholders, including the public.

Although ideas from the rational management model are emphasised in many of the NSI-related documents, such an approach is not without its critics. Criticisms include the inability of management (in terms of analytical skills and time) to operate such a model, the tendency to overemphasise quantitative performance measures and disregard the qualitative and strategic elements in decision making, and the tendency to ignore the political and cultural contexts in which decision making takes place.

Objectives and key findings of the research

The objectives of the empirical studies included in this research report were:

- To identify the degree to which the mission statement, objectives and targets in the corporate and business plans of agencies are consistent, complete and co-ordinated, and the extent to which they are used to provide a basis for external reporting (via the medium of the annual report).
- To identify the perceptions of chief executives of agencies in Northern Ireland in respect of the development, use and impact of mission statements, objectives, targets and performance measures. This aspect of the research represents a case study within the wider UK agency sector.

Matched sets of documents (business plan, corporate plan and annual report) from 24 agencies were analysed. Moreover, interviews with nine chief executives of agencies in Northern Ireland were undertaken. It should be noted that, whereas the analysis of documents covered all UK agencies (including British and Northern Ireland agencies), the interviews focused solely on Northern Ireland agencies. Caution therefore needs to be exercised in 'reading across' the findings from the case-study aspect of the research to British agencies. However, all UK agencies have very similar modes of operation and corresponding concentrations on the importance of targeting and measuring performance. The main findings from the research are as follows.

The evidence of a rigid rational model is weak

It is argued that if a highly rational management approach is being used, then objectives would be clearly linked to a mission statement, each objective would have a number of key targets, and each key target would spawn a number of linked operational targets. Furthermore, all objectives would have targets, and no targets would be unrelated to objectives. The analysis of business and corporate plans shows that this is not the case in the agency sector. For example, using the method outlined in this report, approximately 44 per cent of the objectives in the corporate plans had no related targets, and 23 per cent of the targets (excluding work-programme targets) in the business plans could not be related to objectives. It is suggested that this lack of linkage indicates a possible weakness. For example, if targets are set for activities that are unrelated to objectives, then it is likely that these activities will be emphasised and supported whether or not they further the overall mission of the agency. The evidence from the interviews also suggested something less inflexible than the rational management model as normally described. For example, a sequential process commencing with the formulation of a mission statement and then proceeding to objectives and targets is typically presented. However, in the vast majority of agencies, the sequencing was not rigid and in most cases the chief executive described the process as being iterative.

Chief executives are unaware of the lack of linkages

Although the chief executives acknowledged that at times it was difficult to develop targets for all objectives, the degree of linkage suggested by the chief executives was much stronger than that indicated by the analysis of business and corporate plans. The fact that no deliberate attempt formally to review the links between objectives, targets and performance measures was described, led the researchers to conclude that gaps can arise without the knowledge of the senior management of agencies. This gives rise to a number of concerns similar to those mentioned above. For example, if an objective is stated yet no targets related to that objective are developed, then it is possible, or indeed probable, that activities that support that objective will receive limited attention. These gaps may undermine an agency's attempts to both improve management and provide greater accountability. It is possible that a more formal review of the mission statement, objectives, targets and performance measures within each agency, perhaps with the production of maps internally to support such a process, might avoid these potential adverse consequences.

Relatively, the degree of linkage is greater than in other related studies

The extent of the weaknesses identified above should not be exaggerated. When compared with previous studies in other parts of the wider not-for-profit sector, the results in this study show much greater degrees of linkage. For example, excluding work-programme targets, over 80 per cent of targets could be related to objectives. Such a figure is extremely high when compared with the findings of Brace et al. (1980) and Thompson (1995). This, taken with the maps of individual agencies that are presented in this report, many of which show reasonably tightly coupled sets of mission statements, objectives, targets and performance measures, provides evidence of a significantly greater degree of linkage than is found elsewhere. Indeed, this finding is perhaps of great encouragement to those who advocate the applicability of models of management based on quantification in the agency sector. Given that other studies of the agency sector have suggested that improvements in performance-measurement systems have occurred over time (Hyndman and Anderson, 1998), the relatively high degree of co-ordination presently displayed by agencies may be capable of even further enhancement.

Evidence of flexibility in the systems

A more flexible approach to the concept of rational management than that which is implied by a rigid rational management model is suggested by Tomkins (1987). Although acknowledging the imperfections of a totally comprehensive rational management model, he argues that it is the only model that has a general logic and acceptability to those charged with making progress in the public sector. He highlights the need for rational analysis (that is, the process of identifying cause and effect) where possible, rather than totally rationalistic systems. It could be that, although often articulated in rational management terminology, planning and control systems in the public sector are much more flexible in practical application and are more akin to the logical incremental model (Quinn, 1980). This research provides support for the possibility of this more flexible approach. For example, it could be that, because of the difficulties of identifying cause-and-effect relationships in some agencies, specific targets related to certain objectives are viewed as unhelpful, and judgement is used to interpret results. Moreover, the interviews with chief executives abound with examples of the manner in which mission statements, objectives and targets are developed, and feedback information used, that demonstrate considerable flexibility.

Chief executives perceive major benefits from the use of more rational systems, and limited drawbacks

The chief executives perceived that the importance of rational analysis and performance reporting had increased since agencification and that, overall, this had brought significant benefits. By far the most frequently quoted was the sense of increased focus that it facilitated. Furthermore, all the chief executives believed that this had resulted in benefits to the agency itself, the parent department and the customer. These findings are in line with Karbhari and Pendlebury (1997). Regarding perceived drawbacks, most chief executives were aware of difficulties that had arisen or could arise from an approach that emphasises mission statements, objectives, targets and performance measures. However, there was no impression given of insurmountable adverse consequences, but rather a sense that as problems arose they could be managed.

The key targets in the planning documents provide a basis for the reporting of performance

The empirical studies provide evidence that the targets contained in the planning documents give a basis for the reporting of performance through the mechanism of the annual report. Although there are far fewer performance measures in the annual reports than there are targets in the planning documents, the majority of performance measures are related to targets in the business plans (approximately 64 per cent). Furthermore, it is also clear that it is the key targets of agencies that form the platform for reporting. Over 84 per cent of key targets in the business plans had at least one related performance measure in the annual reports. The interviews with chief executives highlighted an awareness of the importance of key targets in external reporting. The process of discharging accountability gives a visibility to the resources, activities and achievements of an organisation, thus enabling informed discussions and decisions by users. This need to report against key targets encourages management to focus on the issues that are of importance to those stakeholders who are outside the immediate management of the organisation.

1

Introduction

The purpose of this chapter is to outline the background to changes in the UK public sector that have given rise to executive agencies (agencies), and to outline the purpose and structure of the report.

1.1 The changing face of the UK public sector and the emergence of executive agencies

Prior to the 1980s, the emphasis in the UK public sector had been on administration rather than on rational management (which stresses, among other things, quantification). For example, Lindblom (1959) argued that decision making in the public sector was a disjointed activity where individuals and groups adjusted to each other (a partisan mutual-adjustment process) rather than a rational process. Furthermore, budget systems tended to be incremental in nature because of the nature of political institutions, entrenched bureaucracies, the lack of information and the time that would be needed for comprehensive analysis (Wildavsky, 1964). The articulation and application of a more rational approach to public-sector management in the UK occurred primarily in the early 1980s. This has resulted in a shift from issues of policy to issues of management, and the break-up of traditional bureaucratic structures. These changes have been supported by an increasing focus on setting quantitative targets that cover all aspects of an organisation's performance, and reporting in terms related to these targets. It has been suggested that the genesis of this focus can be traced back to the Fulton Report (HM Government, 1968).

One aspect of this focus on rational management was the creation of agencies under the Next Steps Initiative (NSI). The first agency was established as recently as 1988, and by December 1998 there were 138 agencies (113 in Britain and 25 in Northern Ireland), with over 377,000 civil servants (76 per cent of the total) working in such organisations. The main objective of the NSI was to improve performance in the delivery of central-government services in terms other than how much money was spent. This led to a greater concentration on targeting, measuring and reporting performance. It was argued that performance information was necessary to improve management within the public sector and to discharge accountability by the public sector. By having targets (that is, quantified, time-bound objectives) for performance and by measuring achievements against targets, a basis for better management within the public sector is provided. Mayston (1985) suggested that this can help with regard to, among other things, clarifying an organisation's objectives, evaluating the benefits of the service provision, highlighting potential cost savings, and providing a trigger for diagnostic intervention and remedial action. It was argued that performance information, coupled with sound judgement, can lead to improved decisions.

Performance measures can also form the basis for the discharge of accountability by a public-sector organisation. Public-sector organisations are accountable to government and to the public for the resources entrusted to them. These resources are provided with expectations as to actions to be undertaken or results to be achieved. Accountability can be viewed as the requirement to explain or justify what has been done, what is being done, and what has been planned (performance accountability). Although there may be other bases of accountability (for example, for probity in the handling of public funds), the importance of performance accountability has increased significantly in recent years.

These changes can be seen as aspects of NPM[1] (see Hood, 1995), where there has been an increased emphasis on quantification *per se,* specifically in the context of a highly rational model of management behaviour that has been influenced greatly by traditional functional studies of management processes. This can be seen in the HM Treasury (1992) requirement that, for planning and control purposes, agencies should develop targets related to their planned performance, and also in a host of other NSI-related publications. It is argued that this will give direction to their activities and provide a basis for evaluating whether or not they have been effective and efficient. In this scheme, such targets may provide a platform for external reporting and the discharge of accountability. The significance of these issues has increased further with the performance planning and reporting issues in the UK White Paper *Better Accounting for the Taxpayer's Money* (HM Government, 1995). These themes are developed, quite specifically, in more recent NSI-related publications (Next Steps Team, 1995; Cabinet Office, 2000), and more generally by emphasising the importance of performance-related ideas in the *Modernising Government White Paper* (HM Government, 1999).

1.2 The research project

The main objectives of this research project were:

- To review the rationale and difficulties of using a highly rational model of management in the public sector, with its focus on targeting, measuring and reporting performance. This would include an analysis of the movement from a concentration on administration to the adoption of new-style management processes under NPM. A particular emphasis would be placed on the need to co-ordinate the mission statement, objectives and targets within planning documents, and for these to be consistent with the performance measures used in external reports.
- To identify the degree to which the mission statement, objectives and targets in the corporate and business plans of agencies are consistent, complete and co-ordinated. The extent to which these are used to provide a basis for external reporting (via the medium of the annual report) would also be investigated.

- To identify the perceptions of chief executives of agencies in Northern Ireland with reference to the development, use and impact of mission statements, objectives, targets and performance measures. This aspect of the research represents a case study within the wider UK agency sector.

Chapters 2 and 3 focus on the first objective. Utilising the NSI literature, a review and discussion of the objectives of the NSI is given. The origins and growth of the sector are reviewed, together with the management structure and the reporting requirements of agencies. A summary of the findings of recent related research is included to provide a context for the empirical research (included in Chapters 5–7). Drawing heavily on the management literature, three models of management in the public sector are reviewed and analysed (rational, incremental and logical incremental) as the basis for a discussion of the rationale and difficulties of using a highly rational model of management with its focus on quantification. Moreover, the accountability of public-sector organisations is discussed, together with the contribution that appropriate targets and performance measures can make to its discharge.

Chapters 4–7 deal largely with the second and third objectives. These contain an explanation of the methods used (Chapter 4) and present the results of the empirical analyses. The analysis of agency corporate and business plans, and annual reports, sought to identify the extent to which mission statements, objectives and targets are co-ordinated, or linked, in a rational manner, and performance information contained in the annual reports of agencies is consistent with the targets included in the planning documents. The results from these aspects of the research are presented and discussed in Chapters 5 and 6. To explore these issues further, Chapter 7 presents the analysis of interviews with chief executives of Northern Ireland agencies. Chapters 2 and 3 provide a normative rationale, albeit disputed by some, for the use of the rational management model in planning and controlling the activities of an agency (or, indeed, any public-sector body) and for reporting performance. Limited empirical evidence exists in respect of practice. The research is a development of previous work by the authors and others (see, for example, Hyndman and Anderson, 1997a; Karbhari and Pendlebury, 1997; Hyndman and Anderson, 1998). It focuses on a relatively small number of agencies (24 in total) and, through the analysis of matched sets of published documents and interviews, gathers detailed data with regard to planning and reporting. It is the first study of its type to link objectives with targets, and to compare the targets with reported performance measures in annual reports. Overall, it provides detailed evidence of the way in which targets are used in planning and reporting by agencies.

The report is structured as follows:

Chapter 2 outlines the origins and growth of the agency sector since the Efficiency Unit's (1988) report to the Prime Minister. The management structure and reporting requirements of an agency are explained, and the key government objective of performance improvement is highlighted. Moreover, it also reviews three recent research projects with respect to agencies that are related to the empirical studies presented later.

Chapter 3 reviews the rationale and difficulties of using a highly rational model of management in the public sector, with its focus on targeting, measuring and reporting performance, and presents possible alternative models (incrementalism and logical incrementalism). The accountability of public-sector organisations is also discussed, together with the contribution that appropriate targets and performance measures can make to its discharge.

Chapter 4 outlines the methods used in the empirical analyses presented in this report (the results of which are subsequently presented in Chapters 5, 6 and 7). A mixture of quantitative and qualitative research methods is used to address the key research questions.

Chapter 5 presents the results of an analysis of 48 planning documents (relating to 24 agencies) that identifies the extent to which mission, objectives and targets are co-ordinated, or linked, in a rational manner. They are presented, analysed and discussed, with relevant examples used to illustrate the issues.

Chapter 6 presents the results of an analysis of the extent to which performance information contained in the annual reports of agencies is consistent with the targets included in the planning documents (using annual reports from the same 24 agencies analysed in the previous chapter). As before, the results are presented, analysed and discussed. Maps of the mission statements, objectives, targets and performance measures of a number of agencies are provided to illustrate linkages.

Chapter 7 presents the results of a series of interviews with chief executives of agencies in Northern Ireland. These interviews focused on the development, use and impact of mission statements, objectives, targets and performance measures, and were used to obtain a more in-depth understanding of the issues raised in the earlier part of the research report, particularly the empirical studies in Chapters 5 and 6. This aspect of the research represents a case study within the wider UK agency sector.

Chapter 8 details the main conclusions and makes suggestions for further research.

2

The Background to the Next Steps Initiative and a Review of Recent Related Research

This chapter outlines the origins and growth of the agency sector since the Efficiency Unit's (1988) report to the Prime Minister. The management structure and reporting requirements of an agency are explained, the key government objective of performance improvement is highlighted, and the difficulty of measuring public-sector performance is discussed. It also reviews three recent research projects that are related to the empirical work presented later in Chapters 5, 6 and 7. These research projects provide some insight into the nature and breadth of performance targets used in the main planning documents; the use, and trends in use, of performance information in the annual reports; and whether the underlying belief behind the creation of agencies (that is, that giving managers significant freedom to manage their agency would lead to the provision of more effective and efficient services) had been delivered by the NSI programme.

2.1 The origins of agencification and the focus on performance

Many changes have occurred in the public sectors of a number of western countries over the last 20 years. Collectively, these have been referred to as NPM. This is evidenced in the UK public sector by, among other things, the increasing adoption of private-sector managerial techniques, the development of market mechanisms, and the break-up of large units of government into smaller, quasi-autonomous units.

The need to plan, control and report with regard to the performance of public-sector organisations has been a central theme in many UK government initiatives in the last two decades. The Financial Management Initiative (FMI) of 1982 called for managers at all levels in central government to have 'a clear view of their objectives, and means to assess, and wherever possible measure, outputs or performance in relation to those objectives' (HM Government, 1982, p. 5). Similar ideas are included in the NSI, the Citizen's Charter, and developments in education and healthcare. It has been argued that the genesis of this focus can be traced back to the Fulton Report of 1968 (see Carter et al., 1992). This need to measure performance now pervades almost all public-sector management and accounting systems.

Agencies arose following the 1988 report by the Efficiency Unit to the Prime Minister. It argued that the civil service was too large and diverse to manage as a single unit, and that there was a need for smaller, performance-focused units. As a result of this, an extensive programme (the NSI) commenced, with the stated aim of delivering 'government services more efficiently and effectively within available resources for the benefit of taxpayers, customers and staff' (*Next Steps Briefing Note,* April 1996, p. 1).

The main objective of the NSI was to improve the efficiency and effectiveness of the delivery of central-government services. Accountability was widened, and an emphasis was placed on the need to develop performance-measurement and performance-reporting systems. Two key reasons advanced for measuring performance are, firstly, that it provides essential information to improve management within the public sector, and secondly, that it can form the basis for discharging accountability by the public sector. As Carter et al. (1992) state, the development of performance-measurement systems has been 'driven by three sets of linked preoccupations: the control of public expenditure, managerial competence and greater accountability' (p. 180).

The creation of agencies has led to much more visible and identifiable public-service institutions and a much greater emphasis on performance information. A number of NSI publications argue that, to facilitate better management and to improve reporting, there will be a need for more relevant, more timely and more comprehensive information on all aspects of performance. In *The Financing and Accountability of Next Steps Agencies* (HM Treasury, 1989) it was stated that information on performance will 'improve stewardship reporting by Agencies to their responsible Ministers and to Parliament and the wider public' (p. 5). Similarly, in the foreword to *Improving Management in Government: The Next Steps Agencies* (HM Government, 1990), it is stated that the disclosure of more performance information 'has made it much easier to know who to approach to find out about a particular service, to complain, to explain customer needs, or perhaps even to praise' (p. 4).

This discharge of accountability by the provision of performance information (for a fuller discussion of this issue see Hyndman and Anderson, 1998) also has knock-on effects with regard to planning and control systems. While the external reporting of performance information by agencies gives a visibility to the activities and achievements of the organisation, thus enabling informed discussion, it also exerts a pressure on management to improve performance. In considering the overall impact of performance measurement in UK agencies, it has been suggested that 'while obfuscation of performance may suit some managers, the external pressure provided by the disclosure of performance information encourages a focus on performance and provides a catalyst for managers as they seek to achieve performance improvement' (Eden and Hyndman, 1999, p. 13).

These linked themes of performance reporting and planning and controlling to improve performance are continuing thrusts in many of the more recent NSI-related publications (HM Treasury, 1992; Next Steps Team, 1995; Cabinet Office, 2000). Moreover, similar performance-related ideas are contained in the *Modernising Government* White Paper (HM Government, 1999) which focuses on: ensuring that policy-making is more 'joined up' and strategic; the importance of emphasising the needs of public-service users; and the delivery of public services that are of high quality and efficient.

2.2 The growth, structure and reporting of agencies

The first agency was established in August 1988, with three being set up by the end of that year. By the end of 1990, 33 had been established, and four years later the number had grown to 102. Table 2.1 illustrates the significance of the agency sector over the period December 1995 to December 1998.

Table 2.1: The agency sector

Date	*Agencies*	*Other units working on Next Steps lines*	*Civil servants working on Next Steps lines*
Dec. 1995	109	50	366,240
Dec. 1996	129	49	386,225
Dec. 1997	138	50	383,290
Dec. 1998	138	50	377,566

Already-established agencies include the Social Security Benefits Agency (66,296 employees), HM Prison Service (39,363 employees), Historic Scotland (627 employees) and the National Weights and Measures Laboratory (48 employees). Furthermore, by December 1998 another 19 candidates for agency status had been announced.

Agencies work within structures developed by government. The NSI has not changed the normal requirement of ministerial accountability to Parliament. However, the changes build on the conventional relationships between ministers and those carrying out the executive functions of government. The objective is that operational responsibilities be clearly delegated, with the chief executive of each agency being personally responsible to the minister for the management and performance of the agency.

A published framework document is developed for each agency that typically covers such matters as the aims and objectives, reporting and accountability, and the financial and accounting arrangements. Each agency is required to produce a corporate plan, typically covering a three- to five-year period, with annual business plans being developed from this base. Performance targets, financial projections, assessment of prospects and other information are included in the plans, which are developed by the agency in consultation with the department/minister responsible. These may not be published if an agency operates in a competitive market or if there are other operational reasons for maintaining confidentiality (for a fuller explanation see *Next Steps Review 1995*, HM Government, 1996). All agencies are required to produce an annual report and accounts for each year of operation, which provide information on issues such as the agency's financial performance and its achievements against key targets. Such a report is available to all stakeholders, including the public.

2.3 Performance and the public sector

The issue of performance improvement is central to the NSI, yet the concept of what constitutes performance is rather problematical in the public sector. If the performance of an organisation is viewed in terms of the usual production model consisting of three stages (inputs, outputs and results), performance can be judged in terms of efficiency and effectiveness. Effectiveness is the relationship between an organisation's outputs/results (for ease of use this will merely be referred to as outputs) and its objectives, while efficiency is the ratio of outputs to inputs, or the amount of output per unit of input (for a fuller explanation of these terms see Chapter 6). With both business enterprises and public-sector organisations there is a consensus regarding the importance of performance information in meeting the information needs of a variety of users (ASC, 1975; FASB, 1980; ICAS, 1988).

However, a major difference between a public-sector organisation, or any not-for-profit organisation (NFPO), and a business enterprise is that of entity purpose. A business has a profit objective whereas a public-sector organisation generally does not. It is argued by Anthony (1980) that in businesses both the inputs and the outputs can be measured in money terms. Furthermore, because the overall objective is profitability, then profitability, the difference between inputs (expenses) and outputs (revenues), is useful for evaluating efficiency and effectiveness. With most public-sector organisations there is no corresponding monetary measure of output, except to the limited extent that revenue is earned from the sale of services, and often no profit objective. Therefore, the 'profit' figure does not have the same meaning. In public-sector organisations, where multiple, non-financial objectives often exist, it may be difficult to measure output and therefore difficult to evaluate performance.

This is not to say that profit is a perfect measure of performance in a business organisation, or that non-financial measures are unimportant. Monetary measures do not cover all aspect of inputs and outputs. Profit figures are capable of manipulation and focus on the short run, and businesses may have wider objectives than merely profit. Non-financial issues such as customer satisfaction and quality may be important, and these could be key determinants of long-term success. For example, Kaplan and Norton (1996) promulgate the importance of non-financial measures to support long-term profitability objectives. However, it is likely that profit measures will be important in the evaluation of success, especially in the short term. Stewart and Walsh (1994, p. 46) argue, when commenting on business organisations, that 'it is profit that is the final output ...there are universally accepted abstract performance measures, such as return on capital, available'. In public-sector organisations the relevance of 'profit' or 'surplus' is different. Non-financial goals and objectives often dominate, and the political dimension makes rational economic decision-making models less relevant. In these cases, it may be particularly difficult to measure output and therefore difficult to evaluate performance. As Stewart and Walsh comment with respect to profit measures and businesses, 'such simple, unequivocal measures are neither available nor appropriate in the public sector' (p. 46). A fuller discussion of the inherent difficulties of measuring performance in the public sector is provided by Likierman (1993) and Hyndman and Anderson (1997b).

A further complication arises in public-sector organisations in identifying the stakeholders (or users of performance information) and the information that they require. The Government Accounting Standards Board (GASB, 1987) highlights three groups as primary users of public-sector organisations' reports: the citizenry, legislative and oversight bodies, and investors and creditors. Similar lists have been provided by other writers (ASC, 1975; Anthony, 1978; FASB, 1980). However, the application of a user-needs model requires considerable judgement on the part of the information provider. Likierman and Creasey (1985) argue that caution needs to be exercised because of a number of issues, including the imperative to set out the basis for any assertion about needs or rights, the resolution of conflicts that arise when attempting to fulfil such requirements, and the lack of clarity in some of the statements of reporting objectives. Rutherford (1983, p. 22) concludes that although user-needs models provide interesting insights they 'do not yield very rigorous prescriptions for the information to be provided'. These issues are explored further in section 3.2.

2.4 Recent related research in agencies

2.4.1 Hyndman and Anderson (1997a)

Research by Hyndman and Anderson (1997a) has provided some insight into the nature and breadth of performance targets included in the main planning documents of agencies. A total of 83 planning documents (42 business plans and 41 corporate plans) were analysed to identify future target information. The analysis classified future target information into five categories: financial performance, volume of output, quality of service, efficiency, and work-programme targets. The first four categories accord with the subdivisions suggested by HM Treasury (1992), with the fifth category being used to cover targets that relate to the specific achievement of tasks by particular dates. Detailed examples from the plans analysed for each category of target are given in Tables 2.2 and 2.3.

The main findings of the research included the following.

- *The range of targets developed by agencies was not comprehensive*
  A number of agencies failed to disclose at least one target in each category. For example, in respect of corporate plans, 90 per cent of agencies had at least one financial performance target, with the figures for the other categories of targets being 90 per cent (volume), 78 per cent (quality), 76 per cent (efficiency) and 85 per cent (work programme).These percentages were slightly higher in the business plans, with the exception of volume of output targets. Within each target category, a significant number of agencies failed to publish a single target. For example, with regard to quality of service targets in corporate plans, 22 per cent of agencies had no targets. It was argued that, given the increasing articulation by government of the importance of quality, such an omission indicates a deficiency in the breadth of coverage and therefore a lack of balance. Furthermore, it was suggested that without targets in important areas such as quality of service, efficiency, volume of service and financial performance, management's ability to plan and control may be impaired.

Table 2.2: Examples of financial performance and volume targets

Financial performance	
Target	*Agency*
♦ Surplus £3,316,000	♦ Driving Standards Agency
♦ Sale of vehicle registration marks to generate £20m	♦ Driver and Vehicle Licensing Agency
♦ Recover full costs of operations from earnings	♦ Public Trust Office
♦ Complete or sign contracts for improvement and conservation schemes to the value of *c*.£21m	♦ Historic Royal Palaces
Volume	
♦ 373,117 vehicles to be tested	♦ Driver and Vehicle Testing Agency
♦ To place 33,000 people into jobs	♦ Training and Employment Agency
♦ Have a customer base of over 3,600 located in over 27 countries	♦ Defence Clothing and Textiles Agency
♦ 2.4 million visitors to monuments in care	♦ Historic Scotland

Table 2.3: Examples of quality of service, efficiency and work-programme targets

Quality of service	
Target	*Agency*
♦ 93 per cent of company winding-up petitions to be issued within 1 day of receipt	♦ The Court Service
♦ To complete all examinations within 15 weeks	♦ National Weights and Measures Laboratory
♦ 265,000 jobclub places available for people with special needs	♦ Employment Service
♦ Accuracy of 97.9 per cent in handling applications	♦ HM Land Registry
♦ To keep error rates in processing claims below 1.5 per cent	♦ Intervention Board
Efficiency	
♦ Average cost per place £22,276	♦ HM Prison Service
♦ To achieve 2.935 units per post (per day)	♦ HM Land Registry
♦ To achieve a further efficiency saving of 3.2 per cent in real terms	♦ UK Passport Agency
Work programme	
♦ Complete a reappraisal of approx. 10,000 linear feet of records with a view to eliminating low-grade material	♦ Public Record Office of Northern Ireland
♦ To achieve trading fund status	♦ Vehicle Certification

- *The lack of distinction between key and other (non-key) targets may hinder co-ordination*
  Many of the agencies failed to distinguish between key and other (non-key) targets. This was identified as an important distinction by HM Treasury (1992). Restricting the analysis to key targets, the percentage of business plans disclosing at least one financial performance target reduced to 50 per cent, with the figures for the other categories of target being 50 per cent (volume), 67 per cent (quality), 64 per cent (efficiency) and 60 per cent (work programme). The comparable figures for corporate plans were considerably lower across all categories of targets. For example, only 24 per cent of the corporate plans included at least one volume of output target, compared with 50 per cent of the business plans. It was argued that, given HM Treasury's stress on the importance of key targets and their relationship to other targets an agency may develop, the analysis suggests that agencies fail to adopt HM Treasury guidance. Moreover, this is likely to result in a lack of co-ordination in overall target development and a lack of focus by management.

2.4.2 *Karbhari and Pendlebury (1997)*

The researchers addressed the question of whether the underlying belief behind the creation of agencies in the UK (that is, giving managers significant freedom to manage their agency would lead to the provision of more effective and efficient services) had been delivered by the NSI programme. The perceptions of senior managers were surveyed. This was undertaken in a two-stage process. First of all a postal questionnaire survey was undertaken (75 questionnaires were received) to obtain a broad overview of current practices and developments. Second, in an attempt to obtain a more precise understanding of the impact of agencification, interviews were conducted (21 interviews in eight agencies and one parent department).

The main findings of the research regarding the perceptions of senior management included the following.

- *Managers have more freedom to control and have better information since agencification*
  A clear majority of agency managers perceived that they had more freedom and control over their activities as a result of agencification. Specifically with respect to management accounting developments in agencies, respondents felt that there had been an increase in the level of autonomy over budget preparation and monitoring against budget, and there was also general agreement that the quality of management accounting had increased. Most respondents expressed the view that prior to agencification effective budget preparation and budgetary control was non-existent. This is not to say that weaknesses were not perceived, as a number of respondents expressed concern with respect to the timeliness and relevance of budgetary control reports. However, it was clear that a majority of agency senior managers felt that, as a result of the agency programme, they are providing a more effective service and giving increased value for money.

- *A participative approach to setting and monitoring performance targets is used*
  The surveys indicated a large degree of flexibility with regard to setting and monitoring performance targets. Approximately half of the respondents to the questionnaire reported that performance indicators were set in partnership with parent departments, with 21 per cent expressing the view that primary responsibility rested with the agency itself. Performance indicators were generally set within the context of the annual business plans of the agencies and were subject to approval by individual boards (or steering committees) of agencies. With reference to monitoring targets, well over half of those interviewed revealed that primary responsibility rested with the individual budget-holders.

- *Non-financial targets were most favoured by agency managers, although financial targets were most important*
  Although non-financial indicators were preferred, and most frequently used, financial targets were perceived as the most important. In particular, senior managers of agencies sensed that financial performance is really what matters and that assessments of their personal performance are significantly affected by their ability to meet such targets.

2.4.3 Hyndman and Anderson (1998)

The research sought to identify the type and extent of the reporting of performance information in the annual reports of agencies and the change over time. Four sets of agency annual reports, covering different time periods, were collected and analysed. These related to the first annual reports published by agencies during or before the period 1990/91, and the 1991/92, 1992/93 and 1993/94 annual reports. It was stated that many studies of performance in the public sector conclude that efficiency and effectiveness are the two main criteria for judging performance. In considering these aspects of performance, it is common to use a simple production model of the operation of an organisation. The model used in the research was based on a simple three-stage taxonomy capturing inputs, outputs and results (the component parts of performance). This permitted efficiency to be measured by relating inputs to outputs or results (efficiency), and effectiveness to be measured by relating outputs or results to the objectives and targets. Efficiency and effectiveness were referred to as the higher measures of performance.

The initial analysis classified the information into five main types: inputs, outputs, results, efficiency and effectiveness. The percentage of agencies disclosing any effectiveness or efficiency information by year is shown in Table 2.4. The average number of measures, classified into three groups comprising the component parts of performance as group one, efficiency as group two and effectiveness as group three is shown in Table 2.5.

Table 2.4: Information content – efficiency and effectiveness

	Efficiency				**Effectiveness**			
	First annual reports	*1991/92 annual reports*	*1992/93 annual reports*	*1993/94 annual reports*	*First annual reports*	*1991/92 annual reports*	*1992/93 annual reports*	*1993/94 annual reports*
No. of annual reports	29	57	71	88	29	57	71	88
Percentage disclosing at least one measure	38	58	54	57	59	86	94	92

Table 2.5: Information content – average number of performance disclosures per annual report*

	First annual reports	*1991/92 annual reports*	*1992/93 annual reports*	*1993/94 annual reports*
Inputs, outputs and results	8.99	5.18	5.95	10.05
Efficiency	1.03	1.63	1.61	2.09
Effectiveness	3.83	6.75	7.60	7.09
Total	13.85	13.56	15.16	19.23

* Average calculated by dividing total number of measures by total number of reports

The main findings of the research included the following.

- *A significant proportion of agencies fail to report on important aspects of performance*
  This study found that there was a significant proportion of agencies reporting little or no information on efficiency and effectiveness in their annual reports. Although there had been some improvement over time, 43 per cent of agencies did not report a single measure of efficiency in their 1993/94 annual reports. The comparable figure for measures of effectiveness was 8 per cent. It was argued that, given the explicit call by government for agencies to publish information on performance, failure to publish measures of efficiency and effectiveness points to an agency sector where accountability is not discharged in an adequate manner.

- *The reporting of performance has improved over time*
  Notwithstanding the above, the number of performance disclosures per annual report, as measured by the performance model used in the research, increased in total by approximately 40 per cent over the four accounting periods considered, from 13.85 in the first annual reports to 19.23 in the 1993/94 annual reports. The study showed an increased emphasis in the later annual reports in

respect of the use of the higher measures of performance (that is, efficiency and effectiveness). These changes were viewed as improvements, and it was argued that they possibly suggest an evolution of performance reporting.

3

Rational Management, Planning, Control and Accountability

The NSI stresses ideas from the rational management approach and highlights the need to co-ordinate the mission statement, objectives and targets within planning documents. Furthermore, it emphasises the need for targets to be consistent with the performance measures used in external reports. Two key reasons suggested for targeting and measuring performance in the public sector are, firstly, that they provide essential information to improve management within the public sector and, secondly, that they can form the basis for discharging accountability (Carter, et al., 1992; Hyndman and Anderson, 1997b). This chapter reviews the rationale and difficulties of using a highly rational model of management in the public sector, with its focus on targeting, measuring and reporting performance, and presents possible alternative models (incrementalism and logical incrementalism). It is seen that these three models do not define precisely how planning takes place in organisations, but rather represent typical tendencies in planning. In addition, the accountability of public-sector organisations is discussed together with the contribution that appropriate targets and performance measures can make to its discharge.

3.1 Approaches to planning and control in the public sector

3.1.1 Rational management

Many of the UK government publications (see, for example, HM Government, 1982; HM Treasury, 1992; HM Government, 1999) related to planning and control in the public sector resonate with the ideas of rational management promulgated by such writers as Drucker (1954) and Argenti (1989). Key themes connected to such an approach are that strategy should come about by highly systematised forms of planning, and that there is a need for specific and quantified targets.

Many writers from the 1950s onwards promoted the importance of the development of a strategy for an organisation through a sequence of analytical and evaluative procedures. This is often referred to as the rational management model. According to Chandler and Plano (1988, p. 127), this model 'defines the problem, develops alternative solutions, places values on the consequences of various alternatives, assesses the probability that they will occur, and makes a decision based on logical rules'. The emphases of this approach frequently include a 'top-down' view with senior management of the organisation determining and directing strategy, the development of a strategy for the organisation as a whole prior to the construction of supporting strategies for individual business units or functions, and individual strategies being evaluated objectively.

Clear objectives are crucial to the rational management paradigm. Ansoff (1979) suggests that businesses pursue objectives (economic, social or environmental) and that they need to follow a rational management approach because of both the uncertainties in the environment and the requirement for a 'common thread' or consistency. Drucker (1954) argued that objectives are needed in every area where performance and results directly affect the survival and prosperity of the organisation. This philosophy was central to the promulgation of the concept of 'management by objectives' (Drucker, 1976), where he highlighted the importance of the feedback loop whereby objectives were set for key functions, performance was measured in the same terms, and managers would use the information to decide whether or not intervention was required. The need for specific and quantifiable objectives in the public sector was highlighted when he identified one of the 'deadly sins' in public administration as 'having a generalised, lofty objective' (Drucker, 1980, p. 104). Similar themes on the need for focus and quantification occur in his writings on managing NFPOs, where he wrote concerning the formulation of a mission statement:

> A mission statement has to be operational, otherwise it's just good intentions. A mission statement has to focus on what the institution really tries to do and then do it so that everybody in the organisation can say, this is my contribution to the goal. *(Drucker, 1990, p. 4)*

Similar emphases on the need to set objectives and measure against these objectives are found in the writings of Argenti. In relation to businesses, he stated that:

> if a company does not know what it wants, it cannot decide how to get it. Many companies do not know and have to be content to drift through their environment reacting only to stimuli so painful that they just have to do something to stop it hurting. *(Argenti, 1968, p. 35)*

The same theme was evident in specifically considering non-business organisations (Argenti, 1989). He argued that unless executives in these organisations could devise and verify their corporate objectives, then the organisations should be reformed.

Associated with such ideas would be an objectives–plan–targets–monitor–control process of planning and control. Such an approach is summarised in Figure 3.1. Similar ideas, more specifically related to the design of accounting systems, are contained in the writings of Anthony and Young (1999) where three levels of planning and control (or decision making) within an organisation are identified: strategic planning, management control, and task control. Strategic planning is concerned with the long term and is broad in focus. Management control focuses on the shorter term and is less broad and more detailed than strategic planning. Task control is concerned with day-to-day tasks and is the most detailed of all. The importance of quantified objectives (or targets) in operating a system of planning and control is emphasised. They describe a statement of targets (or objectives) as 'a key element in the management control system of a non-profit organisation' (p. 356).

Figure 3.1: Conventional planning and control paradigm

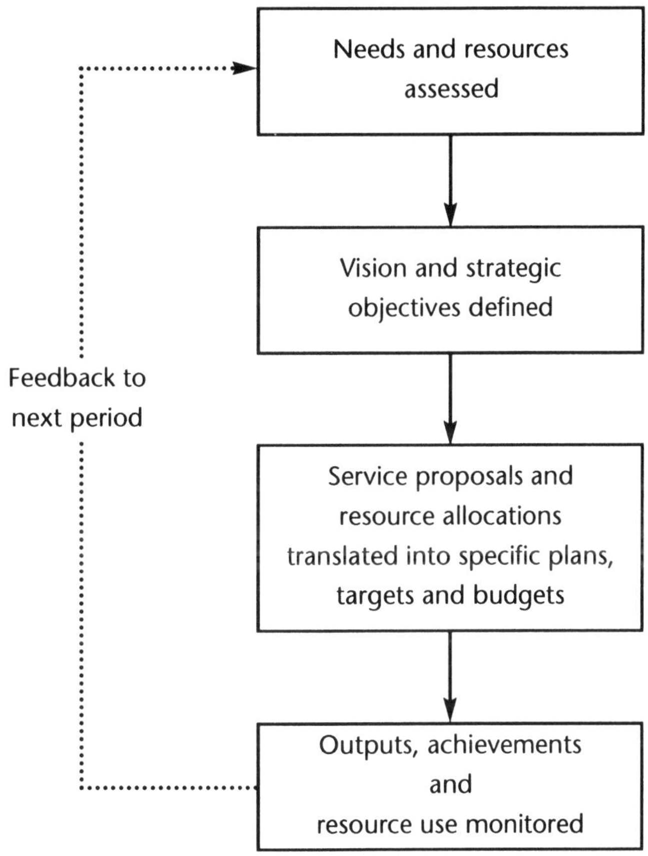

This theme is developed by Mayston (1985) in considering the possible contribution of non-profit performance indicators (NPPIs) in the public sector. Among the potential roles highlighted by Mayston for NPPIs are: to clarify the organisation's objectives; to evaluate the final outcomes; to indicate performance standards; to indicate the effectiveness with which different service activities contribute to each of the dimensions of achievement; to trigger further investigation and possible remedial action; and to indicate areas of potential cost savings. These roles would support the planning and control system outlined in Figure 3.1.

The importance of the linkages between the various levels of planning and control is emphasised by these and other writers. For example, Meekings (1995) argues that performance measures that are implemented and used properly can have a significant impact, and suggests a performance-measurement framework consisting of three key elements which facilitate co-ordination: a top-to-bottom measurement architecture, a systematic review architecture, and an integrated planning and budgeting process. Similarly, Kaplan and Norton (1996) promote the idea of a 'balanced scorecard' which translates mission and strategy into tangible objectives and measures, both for businesses and for not-for-profit organisations. They also argue (p. 10) that such a measurement approach will facilitate the co-ordination of the strategy, objectives and targets by allowing the organisation to:

1. Clarify and translate vision and strategy;
2. Communicate and link strategic objectives and measures;
3. Plan, set targets, and align strategic initiatives;
4. Enhance strategic feedback and learning.

Vinzant (1996) argues that strategic planning is only useful if it impacts at the lower levels in the organisation and becomes a guide for day-to-day operations. Similarly, DuPont-Morales and Harris (1994) highlight the importance of developing clear links between longer-term strategic plans and shorter-term budgets. They state that 'linking strategic planning and performance measurement to the budget process creates a strong system of accountability' (p. 231). This could be accomplished by developing targets regarding the long-term outputs and inputs in the light of the broad strategies of the organisation. This may then provide the basis for the formulation of annual budgets, covering not only expenditure but also outputs, quality of service and efficiency. These overall budgets, broken down into programme or departmental budgets as appropriate, and profiled on a month-by-month basis, could then provide the basis of a system of regular monitoring and afford the opportunity for corrective action.

3.1.2 Criticisms of the rational management approach

A number of writers have criticised the rational management approach. The criticisms are often related to the inability of management (in terms of analytical skills and time) to operate such a model, to the tendency to overemphasise quantitative performance measures and disregard the qualitative and strategic elements in decision making, and the tendency to ignore the political and cultural context in which decision making takes place. To such writers the rational management model is sometimes seen as a 'straw man'.

The idea that management has clear objectives and is perfectly aware of all possible options, and the degree of certainty of each in terms of likelihood of achieving the objectives, is questioned. Chandler and Plano (1988), when considering public-sector organisations, state that managers 'rarely have the brains and never have the time to complete the laborious steps of analysis involved' (p. 132). A related problem regarding the rational management approach is that too much detailed information will be gathered and analysis will then prove to be difficult or impossible. Johnson and Scholes (1999, p. 54) suggest that: 'strategic planning can become over-detailed in its approach, concentrating on extensive analysis which, while sound in itself, may miss the major strategic issues facing the organisation....This can result in information overload with no clear outcome.'

There is also a danger of overemphasising quantitative measures and de-emphasising, or ignoring, the qualitative factors in decision making. This has been highlighted by Earl and Hopwood (1980), who suggest that too much reliance by management on formal channels of communication (possibly including quantitative measures of performance) and mechanistic responses to the information provided may be inappropriate. They argue that in many organisations, especially those with high uncertainty about objectives and unclear cause-and-effect relationships (which are typical circumstances for many public-sector organisations), there is a need for less formal channels of information processing and greater use of subjective judgement. Similar ideas are contained in Emmanuel et al.'s (1990) distinction between programmed and non-programmed decisions. Whereas programmed decisions have a clear input–outcome relationship, non-programmed decisions are subject to uncertainty about their outcomes. In the latter case, greater subjective judgement and reliance on information other than that provided through formal channels is required. This danger is also emphasised by Johnson and Scholes (1999, p. 54), who state that planning 'can become obsessed with the search for absolute determinants of performance' and suggest the need to use a more flexible approach.

The cultural and political aspects of decision making, which are at least as relevant in public-sector bodies as in businesses, are largely disregarded in the rational management model. The relevance of this issue is discussed by Chandler and Plano (1988, p. 127), who state that rational management models 'typically do not take into account the process of conflict, negotiation, persuasion, and co-operation among the private and public groups, institutions and individuals with stakes in particular policies and decisions'. Assumptions of 'objectivity' and 'rationality' ignore such factors. However, Johnson and Scholes (1999, p. 53) suggest that if management is to be successful then 'the cultural and political dimensions of organisations have to be taken into account'.

3.1.3 Incrementalism

A number of writers have been fairly sceptical as to whether or not the wholesale application of the principles of the rational management model can be applied to the public sector. Dearlove (1979) presents a critical and comprehensive analysis of the arguments for moving from 'traditional administration' to 'corporate management'. He is highly critical of the way in which rational management approaches are articulated as the necessary replacements for systems of traditional administration (systems where there is a stress on the importance of law and the inevitable emphasis upon formal structures and processes). As he argues (p. 161):

> Like it or not,... goals are complicated, muddled and ill-defined; motivation is a problem that cannot be assumed away; conflict and politics are everyday features of organisational life; and even managers have capacities far below the duties that are thrust on them by classical theorists. It is a dangerous illusion to believe that a crisp and effective division of labour can be co-ordinated around the organisational objective.

Dearlove's ideas are complemented by Butani (1966) and Hood (1995, 1996). Butani argues that the needs of administration and management in the public sector are sometimes not understood by advocates of change, and comments that 'often one encounters situations where a lot of helter-skelter activity is generated to solve administrative problems of which there is no real and genuine perception' (p. 612). Hood states that it is difficult to sustain the arguments that rational management (as part of NPM) should replace traditional systems of public administration and is applicable to all public-sector settings. Moreover, he takes the view that there is little evidence to suggest that it is, or should be, the new 'global paradigm' in public administration.

An alternative model of how strategy may be developed, or decision making may take place, is the incrementalist approach. Chandler and Plano (1988, p. 128) explain it in this way:

> The incrementalist decision-making sequence calls upon the decision maker to (1) identify the problem; (2) investigate how similar problems have been handled in the past; (3) analyse and evaluate a few solutions that appear to be plausible; and (4) choose one that makes some contribution to solving the problem without drastically altering existing processes and institutions.

Such an approach is based on the belief that the rational model cannot be applied in practice because managers are limited by time, by the information they have and by their own skills, habits and reflexes (what Simon (1976) refers to as 'bounded rationality'). In reality, managers do not optimise, rather they satisfice. Managers carry on searching until they find an option that appears to be tolerably satisfactory, and adopt it, even though it may be less than perfect.

Incrementalism is most associated with Lindblom (1959), where he described it as 'the method of muddling through' (p. 81). He argues that comprehensive rational planning is impossible, and likely to result in disaster if actively pursued. It is suggested that in the real world strategic managers do not evaluate all the possible options open to them in a given situation, but choose between a few alternatives. Furthermore, strategy making involves small-scale extensions of past policy (incrementalism) rather than radical shifts following a comprehensive rational analysis. This is because strategy making necessitates accommodation or compromises with interested groups through political bargaining, a process Lindblom (1965) describes as 'partisan mutual adjustment'. Lindblom argued that the incremental model was to be preferred to the rational model because strategy making involving small-scale extensions of past practices avoids major errors. It is also more likely to be acceptable because consultation, compromise and accommodation are built into the process. Similarly, budgeting systems in the public sector tend to be incremental in nature because of the nature of political institutions, entrenched bureaucracies, the lack of information and the time that would be needed for comprehensive analysis (Wildavsky, 1964). This is despite the fact that arguments have been made for more rational approaches, utilising zero-based budgeting (ZBB) or planning, programming and budgeting systems (PPBS) (see Phyrr, 1973; Stonich, 1977).

Incrementalism also faces severe criticisms. For example, it is argued that incrementalism does not work where radical new approaches are needed. Johnson and Scholes (1999) refer to the need for 'transformational change' at times in an organisation's life where there is a fundamental change in strategic direction. Incrementalism would not facilitate such a change as it has an inbuilt conservative bias. Related to this is the tendency for incrementalism to accept existing methods, structures and processes. Firth and Leigh (1998) saw it as 'the enemy of innovation'. This may be particularly significant when the external environment is changing rapidly and an appropriate strategic response is necessary for survival.

3.1.4 Logical incrementalism

In contrast to 'muddling through', incrementalism can be seen as a purposeful, intentional, and proactive process. Quinn (1980) describes this type of incrementalism as 'logical incrementalism'. Here it is realised that not all options can be identified and analysed. Strategy emerges through a constant process of analysis, re-analysis and modification throughout the development and implementation of strategy in order to keep in line with this environment. It is the deliberate development of strategy by 'learning through doing'. Although the individual stages in the process are managed proactively (Schilit and Paine, 1987), the whole process is not sequentially managed by one individual, nor is the process necessarily orderly, discrete and sequential (Quinn, 1982). Logical incrementalism offers a 'middle way' between rational management and incrementalism. The broad outline of a strategy is developed by an in-depth review, but there remains scope for incremental decision making as the strategy is implemented.

The main difference between incrementalism, as described previously, and logical incrementalism is the sense of logic and rationality in the latter form. Bailey and Johnson (1997, pp. 15–16) argue that organisations that use a logical incremental approach to planning are 'characterised by a clear sense of overall strategic direction, the application and utilisation of planning techniques, and an underlying rationality related to the external environment'. The benefits of such an approach are outlined by Johnson and Scholes (1999). It is suggested that the continual testing and gradual implementation of strategy provides improved quality of information for decision making, and enables the better sequencing of the elements of major decisions. Furthermore, it is argued that such processes take account of the political nature of organisational life, since smaller changes are less likely to face the same degree of resistance as major changes. Moreover, the formulation of strategy in this way means that the implications of the strategy are continually being tested.

Logical incrementalism should not therefore be seen in terms of a neat sequential model. The concept that strategy is the end result of a rational analysis of all possible options does not hold. Logical incrementalism sees strategy as being worked through in action. As Quinn (1980, p. 58) explains, logical incrementalism:

honours and utilises the global analyses inherent in formal strategy-formulation models. It also embraces the central tenets of the political or power-behavioural approaches to such decision making. But it does not become subservient to any one model.

3.2 Targets and accountability

3.2.1 Accountability

Rutherford (1983) considers the need to provide information to users in terms of the concept of accountability. Edwards and Hulme (1995), when discussing non-governmental organisations and 'grassroots' organisations, see accountability as a means by which individuals and organisations report to a recognised authority, or authorities, and are held responsible for their actions. With respect to government organisations, the GASB in its *Concepts Statement No. 1* (GASB, 1987, p. 21) views accountability as the 'paramount objective' in financial reporting and defines it in terms of 'being obliged to explain one's actions, to justify what has been done'. The GASB elaborated on this in a later publication (GASB, 1993, Sec. 100.156) by stating that:

> Governmental accountability is based on the belief that the citizenry has a 'right to know', a right to receive openly declared facts that may lead to public debate by the citizens and their elected representatives. Financial reporting plays a major role in fulfilling government's duty to be publicly accountable in a democratic society.

This concept seems inextricably linked with the contemporary view of accounting, which is seen in terms of providing information to satisfy the needs of users (AAA, 1966; ICAS, 1988). Similar themes occur in discussions on a conceptual framework for financial reporting in the public sector (Mayston, 1992). These writings focus on issues such as the objectives of financial reporting and the information rights and needs of users. In this context, the question arises: to whom is a public-sector organisation accountable? The GASB (1987) highlights three groups as primary users of public-sector organisations' reports: the citizenry, legislative and oversight bodies, and investors and creditors. Similar lists have been provided by other writers (ASC, 1975; Anthony, 1978; FASB, 1980). An examination of these lists shows a common position, where it is accepted that there is a need to report to those outside the immediate management of a public-sector organisation.

Accounting information can provide an important and regular mechanism through which major aspects of accountability are discharged, although, as Jones and Pendlebury (1996) argue, accountability, in its widest sense, is more than accounting (however widely accounting is defined). Yet the application of the concept of accountability (or indeed the user-needs model) is not without problems. Edwards and Hulme (1995, p. 9) suggest that accountability 'is a complex and abstract concept', while the GASB (1987) acknowledges that it suffers from imprecise meaning.

3.2.2 Different bases of accountability

Stewart (1984, p. 16) argues that there are different bases of accountability and states that 'within any field of accountability the bases of accountability must be defined. In relation to the activities for which accounts have to be given, the purpose of the account and hence the basis of accountability can vary.' He then goes on to develop a 'ladder of accountability', relating to public accountability, which contains a number of 'rungs', represented in Table 3.1.

Table 3.1: Stewart's bases of accountability

Base	*Concerned with*
Accountability for probity and legality	Concerned with the avoidance of malfeasance, ensuring that funds are used properly and in the manner authorised, and that the powers given by the law are not exceeded.
Process accountability	Concerned with ensuring that there has been no maladministration and, in particular, no maladministration leading to injustice.
Performance accountability	Concerned with ensuring that there is no waste in the use of resources (efficiency) and, in a wider sense of performance, whether performance achieved meets required standards.
Programme accountability	Concerned with establishing whether a particular organisation has met its objectives; concerned with the work carried on and whether or not it has met the goals set for it.
Policy accountability	Concerned with the policies that the organisation has pursued and those that it has failed to pursue.

Stewart argues that an accountability information system should report on all levels of accountability, and that this will result in a system that reports both financial information, and also output and outcome information. The information needs of each of the user groups (for example, the citizenry, legislative and oversight bodies, and investors and creditors) may be different. For example, the citizenry may be most interested in the results, or effectiveness, of an organisation, whereas the concern of oversight and legislative bodies may be jointly focused on wider performance information, including efficiency, and probity. Investors and creditors may be primarily interested in financial information relating to solvency. In a similar vein, for those groups (including management) with an interest in performance information the measures that are crucial for one group may be significantly less important to another group. As Kanter and Summers (1987, p. 158) highlight:

> Managers might prefer structural measures of organisational characteristics because they have control over such factors; the rank and file might prefer process measures of activities because they control their own performance; and clients and customers prefer outcome measures because they want results, not promises or mere effort.

It has been suggested by a number of writers that there may be a bias towards the discharge of accountability through traditional financial accounts at the expense of wider performance information. It has been argued that a concentration on the provision of traditional financial accounting information may reduce accountability by focusing on the less important (Gibson, 1978; Hedlund and Hamm, 1978; Hyndman, 1990). Gray (1983) argues that financial accounts only fully discharge accountability in the 'special case', the best example of which is the business enterprise/shareholder relationship, and can only go a small way towards discharging accountability in an NFPO.

With reference to most public-sector organisations, it is likely that the need for extensive performance information would be high in order to discharge adequately the accountability of the organisation. Gray (1984, p. 84), in arguing for more disclosure of performance information by charities, expressed the view that 'financial accounts can provide useful additional information. However, the financial accounts can only play a subsidiary role.' In the case of local-government reporting, Boyne and Law (1991, p. 179) argue that in the absence of performance information 'the concept of accountability and indeed the whole democratic process is simply a sham'. A similar theme, although not as extravagantly stated, is found in a GASB-funded research report (Hatry et al., 1990, p. iii):

> the GASB believes that SEA [Service Efforts and Accomplishments] reporting will become a major element of governmental financial reporting, assisting in fulfilling government's duty to be publicly accountable and in enabling citizens, elected officials, and other users of financial reports to assess that accountability.

This process of discharging accountability gives a visibility to the resources, activities and achievements of an organisation, thus enabling informed discussions and decisions. It has been suggested that the need to discharge accountability encourages management to concentrate on the issues that are of importance to those stakeholders who are outside the immediate management of the organisation and often provide the resources for the organisation to function. As has been suggested elsewhere (Eden and Hyndman, 1999), the external pressure provided by the requirement to disclose performance information may encourage a focus for the organisation and provide a catalyst for managers as they seek to improve performance. Fox (1992), making a similar point but in a more negative tone, argues that although accountability is viewed as desirable, empirical investigation commonly indicates that both leaders and subordinates in organisations seek to avoid accountability. Building on this idea, Edwards and Hulme (1995, p. 9) assert that the absence of accountability 'begins to make the likelihood of ineffective or illegitimate actions by an organisation much more probable'. A more extreme version of this argument suggests that in NFPOs with weak forms of accountability there may be no incentive to manage efficiently, and managerial shirking will result (see Hansmann, 1996).

The linkages between the planning system and the discharge of accountability are clear. Although a rational management approach (and, to a lesser extent, a logical incremental approach) would stress the importance of objectives and targets in supporting management as they plan and control the operation of an organisation, such objectives and targets could also provide the basis for the discharge of performance accountability. As Hyndman and Anderson argue (1997b, p. 46), 'a well-developed set of objectives and targets can provide a valuable basis for the discharge of accountability'. Developing this line of argument from the immediately preceding discussion would suggest that a clearly articulated planning and control framework would facilitate the discharge of accountability, whereas an explicit demand for the discharge of accountability would encourage the development of a clearly articulated planning and control framework.

4

Methods Used in Empirical Analyses

This chapter outlines the methods used in the empirical analyses presented in this report (the results of which are subsequently presented in Chapters 5, 6 and 7). As highlighted in Chapter 1, key objectives of the research report included the conducting of empirical research to:

- Identify the degree to which the mission statement, objectives and targets in the corporate and business plans of agencies are consistent, complete and co-ordinated.
- Ascertain the extent to which mission statements, objectives and targets are used to provide a basis for external reporting via the medium of the annual report.
- Establish the perceptions of chief executives of agencies with regard to the development, use and impact of mission statements, objectives, targets and performance measures.

A mixture of quantitative and qualitative research methods is used to address the key research questions.

4.1 Method used to establish the linkages between mission, objectives and targets

Detailed analysis of the individual corporate and business plans of agencies was conducted in order to ascertain the degree to which the mission, objectives and targets are linked in a co-ordinated manner. The objectives of the analysis were achieved by identifying the mission, objectives, key targets and other (non-key) targets in the corporate plans and business plans of agencies, and by identifying links by individual agency. This allowed for a number of research questions to be addressed, including: are there targets for each objective?; are all targets related to objectives?; and are the linkages (if any) clearer for key targets? If a highly rational (rigid) management approach is being used, a tight coupling between levels and a clear cascading of objectives and targets down the organisation would be expected. The objectives would be clearly linked to the mission statement, each objective would have a number of key targets, each key target would spawn a number of linked operational targets, and targets would not be set that were not linked to objectives.

Business plans and corporate plans were requested from all agencies in existence by March 1997 (a total of 130). A significant number of these agencies were unwilling to supply the information for reasons of confidentiality and fewer than 50 of each document were received, with approximately half of this number of agencies supplying both documents which related to the same period. This response rate was similar to Hyndman and Anderson's (1997a) previous request for such information where it was suggested that, even allowing for the fact that a relatively small proportion of agencies are close to operating in a fully commercial environment, such a non-disclosure rate appears high. It was suggested that some agencies, regardless of the importance of confidentiality, prefer their plans to remain outside the public domain, which is contrary to the spirit, and perhaps even the letter, of the NSI. The research was concerned with identifying links between mission, objectives and targets in each agency; therefore, only those agencies that supplied both a business plan and a corporate plan were included in the analysis.[2] A total of 24[3] agencies were analysed.

Forty-eight documents were analysed to identify the mission, objectives and targets in each, and the relationships between them, if any. The absence of generally accepted definitions of terms was a potential problem with the analysis. To reduce difficulties in this area, and thereby reduce subjectivity, a number of steps were taken. A set of definitions was developed in order to ensure that terms were being used in the same way for each agency. In addition, a set of rules of classification was written to deal with common difficulties of analysis. Moreover, two individuals, using the agreed framework, independently and separately conducted the analysis before discussing and agreeing the results. This approach was similar to that used previously by Hyndman and Anderson (1997a).

The corporate plans were analysed to identify the mission (a generalised statement of the organisational purpose, or a statement of the long-term focus of the organisation) of the agency, objectives (statements of intended output in broad terms, not quantified and not time-bound) and targets (quantified, time-bounded objectives). The targets were further subdivided into key targets and non-key targets. The information was then analysed to establish links between the various levels. This was done by each researcher independently on the basis of their understanding of the mission and activities of each agency, having read both planning documents, before discussing any contentious issues and agreeing results. An identical approach was used regarding the business plans, except that it was assumed that the mission (or goals) and objectives of the agency as stated in the corporate plan were to be used as the basis for linkages to the business plan targets (if these were not included in the business plans). In the majority of cases both the mission (and goals) and the objectives were repeated in the business plans. In all cases the researchers attempted to be generous in identifying links, even if the links were somewhat tenuous. The results of this aspect of the research are reported and discussed in Chapter 5.

4.2 Method used to establish linkages between targets and the reporting of performance information

To develop the research further, the extent to which the targets developed in the business plans and corporate plans are used to provide a basis for external reporting (via the medium of the annual report) was investigated. Annual reports are recognised as key documents in the discharge of accountability to external users. *The Corporate*

Report (ASC, 1975, p. 16) states that such information packages are 'the primary means by which the management of an entity is able to fulfil its reporting responsibility'. To establish linkages between mission, objectives and targets, business plans and corporate plans relating to the same period were analysed to detect linkages between objectives and targets (as detailed in section 4.1). To identify relationships between the targets and performance information in the annual reports of agencies, annual reports were then requested for the period relating to the plan. For example, if the corporate plan 1994/7 and the business plan 1996/7 were analysed for an agency, the annual report for 1996/7 was requested. All 24 agencies that had provided matched sets of business plans and corporate plans also provided annual reports. This facilitated the investigation of the use of performance information in the annual reports of agencies in terms of its relationship to the targets included in the planning documents. In other words, it allowed the identification of the extent to which the targets included in the planning documents provided a platform for the discharge of accountability through the medium of the annual report.

Twenty-four annual reports were analysed. Each agency included in the previous analysis (the results are presented in Chapter 5) was also included in this analysis (the results are presented in Chapter 6). Therefore, for the research reported in Chapters 5 and 6, there were 24 matched sets of documents (business plan, corporate plan and annual report). As discussed earlier, studies of performance in the public sector often use a simple production model of the operation of an organisation (AAA, 1989; Hyndman and Anderson, 1997b). For example, an elementary three-stage taxonomy capturing inputs, outputs and results could be utilised. Although there are no standardised definitions for the terms inputs, outputs and results, the following explanation may aid understanding. Inputs are the resources used in providing a service (for example, expenditure incurred, number of staff). Outputs are the actual goods or services produced for consumption (for example, number of vehicle inspections, number of students completing a course). Results are concerned with the impact upon clients or situations (for example, change in the level of education, overall level of customer satisfaction with the service).

In this scheme, the two key criteria for judging performance are efficiency and effectiveness. Efficiency is the relationship between inputs and outputs (for example, cost per vehicle inspected, number of cases handled per employee), whereas effectiveness is the relationship between an organisation's outputs (or results) and its targets (or objectives); for example, actual number of passports issued versus planned number. A possible taxonomy of five categories of target is: financial performance, volume of output, quality of service, efficiency and work-programme targets (for more detail regarding this, see Chapter 5). This largely accords with the categories suggested by HM Treasury (1992). It is possible that targets set for inputs, outputs or results could fall into the categories of financial performance, volume of output, quality of service or work-programme targets, and such would permit effectiveness to be evaluated if measurements were taken against these targets. With regard to efficiency targets, actual measurements of efficiency in the same terms as those used in the setting of the target would permit planned efficiency to be compared with actual efficiency. The research was concerned with identifying the extent to which the targets included in the planning documents were used for external reporting.

For analysis purposes, information was considered disclosed if it were highlighted in some way (hard copy) and not contained in the main narrative of the annual report (soft copy). This approach was used by Hyndman (1990) in studies of UK charities and Hyndman and Anderson (1998) with agencies, where it was argued that soft copy was difficult for the user to isolate and use and was often (Hyndman, 1990, p. 298) 'embedded in a mass of subjective comment'. Whereas at one level this is merely a matter of presentation, information that is highlighted and concise was deemed to be significantly more useful in terms of communicating to users. This is particularly the case when the user has limited, or no, powers of interrogation, which may be the case with many of the users of annual reports. In the overwhelming majority of cases, performance information was clearly separate from the main narrative of the annual report.

The annual reports were analysed to identify the number of performance measures per annual report (split between inputs, outputs, results, efficiency and effectiveness). These were then related back (if possible) to the targets in the business plans, distinguishing between key targets and non-key targets. An identical procedure was conducted with corporate plans. As in the method detailed in section 4.1, a number of steps were taken to reduce subjectivity. Sets of definitions and rules of classification were written to ensure common treatment of similar items. As before, the same two individuals, using the agreed framework, independently and separately conducted the analysis before discussing and agreeing the results. To analyse further the linkages within the business and corporate plans (the results are reported in Chapter 5), and between the plans and the annual reports (the results are reported in Chapter 6), diagrammatic representations or 'maps' of individual agencies were constructed. These maps were created by the researchers on the basis of information gathered from the analysis of business plans, corporate plans and annual reports. Again, these were constructed in draft form, independently and separately, before agreeing a final version, and these provide a visual representation of the connection between mission statements, objectives, targets and performance measures. The results of this aspect of the research are reported and discussed in Chapter 6.

4.3 Method used to establish the views of agency chief executives in Northern Ireland

To obtain a more in-depth understanding of the research outlined above, interviews were conducted in nine agencies. These focused on the development, use and impact of mission statements, objectives and targets. Moreover, some of the possible adverse consequences and difficulties of developing and using such systems were explored. Chief executives of agencies were interviewed to identify their perceptions with regard to these issues. This group was chosen because of its seniority, assumed detailed knowledge of the issues, and ability to provide an overview of the entire operation of the agency. Given the difficulties of gaining access to chief executives (which were considerable), the potential sensitivities of the matters being discussed and the desire for them to be as candid as possible, chief executives were informed (prior to agreeing to be interviewed) that interviews would be reported in a manner where specific statements could not be attributed to particular individuals, and that there would be no contact made with the parent department regarding the research. It was considered that such assurances were necessary in order to increase the number of participants and the quality of participation. All the chief executives who were contacted agreed to participate in the research.[4]

The agencies selected for the interview survey were taken from those that had provided documents for the previous research (as above). Additionally, because of the constraints of travel, time and finance, agencies were selected that were reasonably accessible to the researchers (all located in Northern Ireland). The Northern Ireland civil service (NICS) is an example of a separate regional civil service and did not have to adopt the agency model (although custom and practice encourages such adoption). This aspect of the research thus constitutes a case study within the wider UK agency sector. This issue is discussed in more detail in Chapter 7. The interviews were conducted at the agencies' headquarters, which provided the researchers with an opportunity to gather additional information on the nature of the agency and its operations. A semi-structured interview approach, with the use of an interview guide, was utilised (see Appendix), and the interview length ranged from two and a half hours to four hours. Two researchers conducted the interviews, and all the interviewees allowed their interviews to be recorded by tape. To ensure accuracy and comprehension of the interview data at the analysis stage, the tapes were transcribed immediately. Notes were also taken during the interview. The results of this aspect of the research are reported and discussed in Chapter 7.

5

Linkages between Mission, Objectives and Targets

The purpose of this chapter is to present the results of an empirical analysis of business plans and corporate plans of 24 UK agencies (a total 48 planning documents) which identifies the extent to which mission, objectives and targets are co-ordinated, or linked, in a rational manner. The method used in this analysis is detailed in section 4.1.

5.1 Results

The initial analysis identified the mission statement and number of objectives in each corporate plan. The results are given in Table 5.1. As an example, the mission statement and objectives of the Valuation and Lands Agency were:

Mission statement: To be the first choice for professional advice on property and the principal provider of valuation services for the public sector in Northern Ireland.

Objectives:

(i) To deliver services to clients and ratepayers which fully meet their agreed requirements and which are fair, accurate, prompt and helpful.

(ii) To improve the overall efficiency and cost effectiveness of services by increasing productivity and reducing unit costs.

(iii) To manage resources economically and efficiently and develop financial management information systems which facilitate and support the agency's overall objectives.

(iv) To develop management and personnel policies which encourage all personnel to achieve the corporate objectives.

Table 5.1: Mission statement and objectives (corporate plans)

Agencies analysed	24
Number with mission statement	24
Number with at least one objective	24
Total number of objectives	144
Average number of objectives	6
Modal number of objectives	5
Range	2–19

As can be seen from Table 5.1, all the agencies included a mission statement in their corporate plans. The average number of objectives per corporate plan was six, ranging from a low of two (the Driver and Vehicle Licensing Agency, Northern Ireland) to a maximum of 19 (the Disposal Sales Agency). The modal value was five.

Details of the linkages between objectives and targets are presented in Table 5.2, which shows objectives with at least one related target and objectives with no related targets, for both corporate plans and business plans. A number of targets are described as 'key targets', presumably because they were high level or covered critical success areas, so further analysis is included distinguishing between key targets and non-key targets. As can be seen from Table 5.2, 77.1 per cent of objectives have at least one target related to them in the business plans, the figure being 56.3 per cent in the corporate plans. Conversely, approximately 23 per cent and 44 per cent of objectives do not have a single target related to them in the business plans and corporate plans respectively. Examples of objectives with no targets include the Disposal Sales Agency which had an objective 'to encourage customers to provide early notification of surpluses' but no target relating to this, and the Rate Collection Agency which had an objective to 'improve the awareness of ratepayers in the owner-occupied sector of entitlement to Housing Benefit' with no related target. The fact that the percentage of objectives having at least one related target in the business plans is significantly higher than in the corporate plans (77.1 per cent compared with 56.3 per cent) is perhaps unsurprising, given that there were many more targets included in the business plans. In total there were 939 targets in the business plans and 423 in the corporate plans, with 274 and 163 of them respectively described as key (see Table 5.3). In respect of key targets, 56.9 per cent of objectives could be related to at least one key target in the business plans, with the percentage being lower in the corporate plans (31.2 per cent). Again, this is unsurprising, given that the business plans contained many more key targets.

These linkages are explored further by considering this from the reverse direction and identifying whether each of the targets can be linked to an objective. Table 5.3 presents the results of an analysis of all targets to ascertain the extent to which these can be related to objectives. As in the previous table, the data is further analysed to distinguish between key and non-key targets. This shows that 72.1 per cent of the targets in the corporate plans could be related to an objective (or, that conversely, 27.9 per cent could not). The extent to which this relationship can be established was weaker in the business plans, with 64.3 per cent of targets being able to be related to an objective. Table 5.3 also indicates a difference between key and non-key targets. Approximately 85 per cent of key targets (for both types of plan) were related to an objective, whereas the comparable figures for non-key targets were 55.6 per cent (business plans) and 63.5 per cent (corporate plans).

Table 5.2: Objectives having related targets (corporate plans and business plans)

	All targets				*Key targets*				*Non-key targets*			
	BP		*CP*		*BP*		*CP*		*BP*		*CP*	
	No.	%	No.	%	No.	%	No.	%	No.	%	No.	%
Objectives with at least one related target	111	77.1	81	56.3	82	56.9	45	31.2	82	56.9	57	39.6
Objectives with no related targets	33	22.9	63	43.7	62	43.1	99	68.8	62	43.1	87	60.4
TOTAL	144	100	144	100	144	100	144	100	144	100	144	100

Table 5.3: Targets and related objectives (corporate plans and business plans)

	All targets				*Key targets*				*Non-key targets*			
	BP		*CP*		*BP*		*CP*		*BP*		*CP*	
	No.	%	No.	%	No.	%	No.	%	No.	%	No.	%
Targets related to objectives	604	64.3	305	72.1	234	85.4	140	85.9	370	55.6	165	63.5
Targets with no related objectives	335	35.7	118	27.9	40	14.6	23	14.1	295	44.4	95	36.5
TOTAL	939	100	423	100	274	100	163	100	665	100	260	100

Hyndman and Anderson (1997a) classified future target information into five categories: financial performance, volume of output, quality of service, efficiency and work-programme targets. The first four categories accorded with the subdivisions suggested by HM Treasury (1992), with the fifth category being used to cover targets that relate to the achievement of specific tasks by particular dates. Examples of work-programme targets include (all time-bound): installing a new computer system, having in place a training and personal development strategy, achieving trading fund status, and completing the introduction of resource accounting. Forty-nine per cent of all targets reported in this research were of this nature (661 out of 1,362). However, a large proportion of this target category could not be related to an objective (70.4 per cent of all work-programme targets). As Pendlebury et al. (1994, p. 40) suggested, these targets are 'more indicative of internal management processes'. They tend to be related to the development and support of efficient management mechanisms, although, because of the drafting of the objectives in many agencies, not specifically related to any one objective in particular.

To eliminate the possibly distorting effect of such targets in identifying linkages, the previous data relating to targets and their related objectives (Table 5.3) has been reworked to exclude work-programme targets in Table 5.4. This shows that once work-programme targets are eliminated from the analysis the degree of linkage between targets and objectives increases significantly. As can be seen, 88.3 per cent of the targets in the corporate plans can now be related to an objective, with only 11.7 per cent unrelated. Seventy-seven per cent of the targets in the business plans are related to an objective. With regard to key targets the degree of relation is even more pronounced, with 89.7 per cent (business plans) and 95.9 per cent (corporate plans) of targets being related to an objective.

Table 5.4: Targets and related objectives (corporate plans and business plans) excluding work-programme targets

	All targets				*Key targets*				*Non-key targets*			
	BP		*CP*		*BP*		*CP*		*BP*		*CP*	
	No.	%	No.	%	No.	%	No.	%	No.	%	No.	%
Targets related to objectives	349	77.0	219	88.3	201	89.7	118	95.9	148	64.6	101	80.8
Targets with no related objectives	104	23.0	29	11.7	23	10.3	5	4.1	81	35.4	24	19.2
TOTAL	453	100	248	100	224	100	123	100	229	100	125	100

Examples of the linkages between objectives and targets can be seen in Table 5.5. An example of the operation of the method can be illustrated with reference to the Planning Inspectorate. It was deemed that the target '80 per cent of English planning appeals by written representation to be decided within 18 weeks' was linked to the objective 'to provide as efficient, expeditious and economic a service as is compatible with the maintenance of quality and high professional standards'. This was linked because the objective of providing an 'expeditious' service (that is, a speedy and efficient service) was deemed to be related to, and possibly facilitated by, a target based on turnaround time on planning appeals.

Examples of a lack of linkage are shown in Table 5.6. The case of the Army Technical Support Agency can be used to illustrate the method. The target to 'be responsive to *ad hoc* (helpline) technical queries – achieve 80 per cent of queries resolved' etc., could not be related to any one of the three objectives of the agency. These can be summarised as: 1, to reduce whole-life costs by providing technical advice and services; 2, to maintain the capability to deploy technical specialist manpower; and 3, to maximise the efficiency of operations by developing an integrated multidiscipline structure. As can be seen, a quality target related to speed of response to telephone enquiries does not link with any of these objectives. This is not to say that it may or may not be an appropriate target for the agency, but perhaps the objectives need to be revisited to justify its use. With respect to the Defence Clothing and Textiles Agency (see Table 5.6), the work-programme target to 'develop and maintain a proactive human resource policy by April' was unrelated to any of the stated objectives. As highlighted earlier, a significant proportion of unlinked targets related to work-programme targets. This was because the objectives were often stated in fairly high-level terms relating to outputs, whereas work-programme targets tended to be associated with specific tasks often connected to internal management processes (for example, install a new computer system by a particular date). Although, at one level, such targets may support many (or all) objectives, they are nevertheless often unrelated to any particular objective.

Table 5.5: Linkages between objectives and targets

Agency	*Objective*	*Target*
Planning Inspectorate	To provide as efficient, expeditious and economic a service as is compatible with the maintenance of quality and high professional standards.	Eighty per cent of English planning appeals by written representation to be decided within 18 weeks.
Medical Devices Agency	Run its services efficiently and effectively within agreed financial limits and in accordance with the Secretary of State's policies.	Develop programmes to reduce continuously the running cost of those activities not subject to specific cost-recovery targets by 3 per cent this year and 2 per cent per annum thereafter.
Public Record Office	To carry out the programme for improving the preservation of public records.	To increase the proportion of records stored in acceptable storage conditions from 87.75 per cent to 87.85 per cent during the current year and by 0.1 per cent each year thereafter.

Table 5.6: Targets unrelated to objectives

Agency	*Target*
Army Technical Support Agency	Be responsive to *ad hoc* (helpline) technical queries – achieve 80 per cent of queries resolved on receipt or within two working days, with the remaining 20 per cent acknowledged with a plan on how the query will be resolved.
Defence Clothing and Textiles Agency	Develop and maintain a proactive human resource policy by April.
Social Security Agency (Northern Ireland)	Number of National Insurance Surveys for the year: 3,800 (including 1,020 employer educational visits).

5.2 Analysis and discussion of results

The creation of agencies can be seen as one aspect of the application of NPM. Quasi-autonomous units were set up and an emphasis was placed on improving performance by improving management. This has led to a focus on rationalism within the public sector and a greater emphasis on formal planning and control systems. Prominent within this scheme has been the need to develop and link mission statements, objectives and targets. This is seen in the Efficiency Unit's (1988) report, formal guidance on setting targets and measuring performance (HM Treasury, 1992), and a host of other NSI publications.

Criticisms of the application of a rational management approach in the public sector have been made regarding the way in which changes have been made and the feasibility of implementing such changes in the public sector at all. These are sometimes based on evidence illustrating the extreme difficulties of utilising a tightly coupled planning and control system and the possible dysfunctional consequences that may result (Hopwood, 1985; Smith, 1993; Mol, 1996). A more extreme criticism is that calls for the use of a rational management approach have led to a 'lip-service', or ritualistic, response by organisations, because of either an inability to respond or a lack of commitment to the cause (Sharifi and Bovaird, 1995; Thompson, 1995). In both cases, the difficulty of linking the higher-level strategic objectives to lower-level operational targets is seen as problematical.

This research presents empirical analysis of 48 planning documents of agencies to identify the degree of co-ordination between mission statements, objectives and targets. It is argued that if a highly rational management approach is being used (Sharifi and Bovaird (1995) refer to the most extreme application of this as 'complete rationality') then objectives would be clearly linked to a mission statement, each objective would have a number of key targets, and each key target would spawn a number of linked operational targets. Furthermore, all objectives would have targets and no targets would be unrelated to objectives. The evidence in this analysis shows clearly that this is not the case. Forty-four per cent of objectives in the corporate plans had no related targets. The figure was lower for business plans (23 per cent). Moreover, approximately 33 per cent of all targets could not be related to an objective (36 per cent in the business plans and 28 per cent in the corporate plans). Such results point to a lack of linkage in the planning documents of agencies, and possibly a lack of co-ordination and focus. For example, if objectives are stated yet no targets related to that objective are developed, then it is possible, or indeed probable, that activities that support that objective will receive little attention. Conversely, if targets are set for activities that are unrelated to objectives, then it is likely that these activities will be emphasised and supported whether or not they further the overall mission of the agency.

Related work by Hyndman and Anderson (1997a), although not dealing specifically with this issue of linkages, highlighted certain weaknesses in target-setting by agencies, including the limited range of targets being used and a lack of distinction between key and other targets. This research provides a more complete picture of the planning and control practices of agencies by illustrating a lack of linkage between mission statements, objectives and targets. However, the extent of the weakness should not be overstated. Although there is no equivalent previous study of this sector that permits a longitudinal view to be expressed, previous studies in other not-for-profit sectors suggest that developing and co-ordinating objectives and targets is a difficult task (Brace et al., 1980; Thompson, 1995). The results found here show a much greater degree of co-ordination than the findings in these previous studies. For example, Thompson's study, which involved an analysis of the contents of eleven New Zealand local authority reports, found that in 'ten of the eleven reports surveyed no attempt was made to show which performance indicators related to which higher goals of the organisation' (p. 342). The results in this study, although not strictly comparable with the Thompson study, paint a much more positive picture with respect to linkages, with 77 per cent of objectives having at least one related target in the business plans and 67 per cent of all targets related to an objective. Furthermore, a significant proportion of the targets that could not be related to objectives were work-programme targets often relating to the achievement of specific tasks by a particular time. Because objectives are often stated in terms of fairly high-level outputs, many of these targets, which tend to be related to internal management processes, cannot be specifically related to them. Excluding work-programme targets, over 80 per cent of targets were related to objectives.

A more flexible approach to the concept of rational management than that which is implied by a rigid rational management model is suggested by Tomkins (1987). Although acknowledging the imperfections of a totally comprehensive rational management model, he argues that it is the only model that has a general logic and acceptability to those charged with making progress in the public sector. He highlights the need for rational analysis (that is, the process of identifying cause and effect) where possible, rather than totally rationalistic systems. It is argued that, although often articulated in rational management terminology, planning and control systems in the public sector are much more flexible in practical application (indeed, as discussed earlier, some writers view the rational management model as a 'straw man', and argue the case for logical incrementalism in the public sector rather than rational management; see Quinn, 1980). The analysis in this research provides some support for the possibility of this more flexible approach. Although no direct evidence for such a position is provided by this research, it could be that because of the difficulties of identifying cause-and-effect relationships in some agencies, specific targets related to certain objectives are viewed as unhelpful, and judgement is used to interpret results. Support for this argument can be found in the writings of Ouchi (1979) and Earl and Hopwood (1980). This could possibly account for some of the objectives having no related targets. This issue is revisited later when the results of interviews with chief executives of agencies are presented (see Chapter 7).

Associated with the above is the issue of whether one model of management is appropriate to all agencies. The NSI literature extols the virtues, explicitly or implicitly, of a rational management model with its associated tight coupling. Very little attention is paid to context, and it almost appears that there is a view that such a model is appropriate to all agencies: a 'one size fits all' view. Where objectives are unambiguous, and where there are clear cause-and-effect relationships, it may be that a fairly tight coupling between mission, objectives and targets is possible and appropriate. However, where this is not the case, a much looser coupling may be advisable. In these latter cases it is probable that there will be a need to use substantial subjective judgement to supplement feedback information based on quantitative targets. The agency sector is very diverse, with considerable differences in type and size of agency. Already-established agencies include the United Kingdom Passport Office and the National Weights and Measures Laboratory. It is possible that the tightness of coupling in an agency such as the Passport Office, which is responsible for carrying out a number of fairly routine tasks, will be greater than in an agency such as the National Weights and Measures Laboratory, where cause-and-effect relationships, and ultimate outcomes, are significantly less clear. As argued previously, these differences may explain at least some of the objectives having no related targets.[5]

This recognition of differences is not clearly acknowledged in the NSI literature. On a strict interpretation of the literature one would expect all objectives to have related targets. One explanation of the findings in this research could be that the rational management model, although articulated, is not rigorously implemented and policed by departments. An alternative view, and one for which Karbhari and Pendlebury's (1997) research provides some support, is that the application of a rigid, top-down, tightly coupled set of targets and performance measures for agencies to pursue (as would be the case if a rigid rational philosophy were operational) is not found in practice. Rather, something more akin to logical incrementalism is found. What may be the case is that, although formally articulated in terms of a comprehensive rational model of management, in reality there is recognition of the need to understand the context in designing and using systems. The fact that Karbhari and Pendlebury found meaningful discussions taking place between stakeholders before targets were set (rather than imposed, top-down targets) suggests some element of sensitivity to context. The extent of this sensitivity, and whether it is applied with all agencies, is unknown. This difference between the articulated model and the model found in practice may be owing to the dominant emphasis on traditional administration found in the UK public sector prior to 1979. To counteract this legacy, and to bring about a change to a more rational approach, it may have been thought necessary to articulate stridently the rational management model, regardless of whether or not such a model was considered totally appropriate in all settings.

5.3 Concluding comments

This chapter presents results that highlight the way in which agencies co-ordinate (or link) their mission, objectives and targets. From the rational management literature, it would seem that a tight coupling of these aspects of planning and control systems is a necessary prerequisite to effective management. Such a model is stressed in the NSI literature. The empirical research illustrates a degree of linkage between mission, objectives and targets (and therefore a degree of rationality), but much weaker than would be expected if a rigid rational management view were dominant. Therefore the tight rational model, as articulated in the NSI literature, is not comprehensively applied in all agencies. Evidence is found of a degree of rational analysis and a more flexible system than a rigid rational management philosophy would require. Karbhari and Pendlebury (1997) provide some limited support for this view in the agency sector, as do the observations of Tomkins (1987) in the wider public sector.

Notwithstanding the above comments, the research still indicates a significant weakness in the ability of agencies to link objectives to targets. For example, approximately 33 per cent of targets were unrelated to objectives. It was argued that if targets are set for activities that are unrelated to objectives, then it is likely that activities will be emphasised that may not support the mission of the agency. This, coupled with weaknesses identified by Hyndman and Anderson (1997a) who found significant non-use (or non-disclosure) of targets in key areas, suggests that the setting and linking of mission, objectives and targets is deficient in providing the necessary breadth and co-ordination to enhance planning and control. The need for much further work in this area is therefore required if the high-minded goals of the NSI are to be realised.

The review of the applicability of a rigid rational management model to the agency sector suggests that a flexible approach may be more appropriate to certain types of agency, especially those where objectives are ambiguous, and where there are unclear cause-and-effect relationships. Indeed, it could be argued that all agencies demonstrate these features to a greater or lesser extent. However, this does not necessarily mean the abandonment of a system of setting mission statements, objectives and targets, but it does encourage a sensitivity to context and an awareness that the creation of a good system needs creativity and experiment, and possibly renewal over time.

Criticisms of formal systems of planning and control in the public sector, including those relying on the process of quantification and giving prominence to accounting systems, are often made. Some of these criticisms relate to an insensitivity to context and have been referred to above. Others relate to what is seen as the pervasive and all-consuming influence of accounting in inappropriate settings.[6] It appears at times, as Lapsley (1998) comments, that some writers view the pre-1979 era in the public sector as a halcyon period, devoid of problems. This was clearly not the case. The danger is that progress (however defined) will fail to be recognised and systems that can contribute to better management in the public sector will be abandoned. However, even strong supporters of formal planning and control systems in the public sector realise that performance is often a contestable notion and cannot be measured perfectly. For example, Anthony and Young (1999, p. 581) state that 'valid criticism can be made about almost every output measure, since few, if any, are perfect'. They go on to argue that such data can be very valuable to management as long as account is taken of the imperfections.

This research, together with the findings of Hyndman and Anderson (1997a) and Karbhari and Pendlebury (1997), illustrates a significantly more complete and co-ordinated system of planning and control than some studies of other parts of the public sector have suggested (for example, Thompson, 1995; Hopwood, 1985). Furthermore, Carter (1991) posited the idea that in the wider public sector there is an innovation cycle in developing such systems. Similarly, Hyndman and Anderson (1998) present indications that there is improvement over time in the external reporting of performance measures by agencies. Such evidence provides hope for the continuing refinement of planning and control systems from what is a relatively new organisational form.

6

Linkages between Targets and the Reporting of Performance Information

Chapter 5 identified the extent to which mission, objectives and targets included in the planning documents of agencies are co-ordinated, or linked, in a rational manner. This chapter develops the research by presenting the results of an analysis of the extent to which performance information contained in the annual reports of agencies is consistent with the targets included in the planning documents. The annual reports of the same 24 agencies analysed in Chapter 5 are used as the basis for the analysis. In addition, 'maps' of the mission, objectives, targets and performance measures of a number of agencies are provided to illustrate linkages. A detailed explanation of the method used in this aspect of the research appears in section 4.2.

6.1 Results

The performance information in the 24 annual reports was analysed and related to the targets in the corporate plans and business plans. Initially, the analysis focused on the targets in the planning documents (as reported in Chapter 5) and whether a performance measurement capturing the essential ingredients of the target was included in the annual report relating to the relevant planning period. For example, if the business plan for 1996/97 had a target of providing a particular service within five days of a request, the annual report was analysed to identify whether a performance measurement relating to the time taken from initial request to provide that service was reported. In this way, the extent to which the targets included in the planning documents provided a platform for reporting the performance of the agency could be established. Details of the linkages between the targets in the corporate plans and the performance measures in the annual reports are shown in Table 6.1, with the same information for business plans shown in Table 6.2. These show targets included in the plans that have at least one related performance measure in the annual report, and targets with no related performance measure in the annual report.[7] As indicated previously, a number of the targets are described as key targets, and the tables distinguish between key targets and non-key targets.

As can be seen in Table 6.1, of the 423 targets in the 24 corporate plans only 34.8 per cent of them (147) were related to a performance measurement used in the annual report. The difference between key targets and non-key targets was striking, with 67.5 per cent of the key targets (110) having a related performance measurement in the annual report compared with only 14.2 per cent of non-key targets. This pattern is even more pronounced with respect to the business plans. As indicated in

Chapter 5, there were many more targets in the business plans (939 compared with 423). A similar proportion of all targets in the business plans (32.3 per cent) could be related to a performance measurement in the annual report (compared with 34.8 per cent of corporate plan targets). However, 84.7 per cent of business plan key targets (232) could be related to a performance measurement compared with only 10.7 per cent of non-key targets.

The linkages between targets in the planning documents and performance measurements in the annual reports are further explored by considering the situation from the reverse. Table 6.3 presents the results of an analysis of all performance measures included in the annual reports and the extent to which they can be related to targets in the planning documents, again distinguishing between key and non-key targets. The number and percentage of performance measures having a related target in the corporate and business plans is reported in Table 6.3.

Table 6.1: Corporate plan targets having related performance measures in the annual reports

	All targets		*Key targets*		*Non-key targets*	
	No.	%	No.	%	No.	%
Targets with at least one related performance measure	147	34.8	110	67.5	37	14.2
Targets with no related performance measures	276	65.2	53	32.5	223	85.8
TOTAL	423	100	163	100	260	100

Table 6.2: Business plan targets having related performance measures in the annual reports

	All targets		*Key targets*		*Non-key targets*	
	No.	%	No.	%	No.	%
Targets with at least one related performance measure	303	32.3	232	84.7	71	10.7
Targets with no related performance measures	636	67.7	42	15.3	594	89.3
TOTAL	939	100	274	100	665	100

As can be seen in Table 6.3, of the 441 performance measures identified in the 24 annual reports, 144 of them (32.7 per cent) could be related to a target in the corporate plans. Conversely, 297 of the performance measures could not (67.3 per cent). Of the 144 related performance measures, 77.1 per cent of them were related to a key target in the corporate plan. The extent to which linkages existed between the performance measures in the annual reports and targets in the business plans was considerably stronger. Table 6.3 shows that 281 of the performance measures included in the annual reports (63.7 per cent) could be related to a target in the business plans and only 160 (36.3 per cent) could not. Of these 281 performance measures that could be related to targets in the business plans, 216 of them (76.9 per cent) were related to key targets. This difference between the corporate plans and business plans is perhaps unsurprising, given that the annual reports matched the exact time period of the business plans (one year), rather than the longer time horizon covered by the corporate plans (usually three years).

Table 6.3: Performance measures in the annual reports having related targets in corporate and business plans

	Corporate plans		*Business plans*	
All performance measures	*No.*	*%*	*No.*	*%*
Performance measures related to targets	144	32.7	281	63.7
Performance measures with no related target	297	67.3	160	36.3
TOTAL	441	100	441	100
Related performance measures:				
Related to key targets	111	77.1	216	76.9
Related to non-key targets	33	22.9	65	23.1
TOTAL	144	100	281	100

Examples of the linkages between targets and performance measures are presented in Table 6.4. For example, the Social Security Agency had a target to recover income support overpayments and reported its achievement in exactly the same terms as the target. Similarly, the Rate Collection Agency had a target to reduce rating debt as a percentage of the gross collectible rate and reported performance in the annual report in identical terms.

Table 6.4: Linkages between targets in the planning documents and performance measures in the annual reports

Agency	*Target*	*Performance Measurement*
Rate Collection Agency	To reduce rating debt to 1.83 per cent of the gross collectible rate.	Rating debt reduced to 1.77 per cent of the gross collectible rate.
Social Security Agency	To recover £1.7 million of income support overpayments.	£2.2 million of income support overpayments recovered.
Training and Employment Agency	To reduce administration costs by more than 3 per cent.	Administration costs reduced by 11.9 per cent.

6.2 Examples of maps of individual agencies

To illustrate further the extent of the linkages in individual agencies, maps (diagrammatic representations of the linkages between mission statement, objectives, targets and performance measures) of five agencies are presented. As indicated in Chapter 4, these maps were created by the researchers on the basis of information gathered from the analysis of business plans, corporate plans and annual reports, as reported in Chapter 5 and earlier in this chapter. It should be emphasised that there was no evidence in these documents (or in the interviews with chief executives reported in Chapter 7) that such maps were constructed by agencies for their own use. The information provided is indicative of the nature of the co-ordination occurring in individual agencies. For each agency a short explanation of the agency and its documents is given and a map is presented. As discussed previously, it has been argued that a well-structured and comprehensive set of targets can provide a useful basis for discharging accountability through the medium of the annual report.

6.2.1 Meat Hygiene Service

A map of the Meat Hygiene Service is given in Figure 6.1. The Meat Hygiene Service was formed as an executive agency of the Ministry of Agriculture, Fisheries and Food in 1995, and is responsible for enforcing hygiene, inspection and welfare regulations in licensed fresh meat plants in Great Britain. Its mission is 'to be a service which has the full confidence of all its customers, including the meat industry, consumers and ministers, through the achievement of improving standards and increasing efficiency'.

In the planning documents analysed, there were five objectives (as shown in Figure 6.1). As can be seen, each of these objectives had at least one associated target (in fact, each objective had at least one key target), and there were a number of non-key targets (mainly work-programme targets). Each of the targets could be related to an objective. In respect of performance information in the annual report, all key targets were reported on but none of the non-key targets (all the targets illustrated in the map of the Meat Hygiene Service are key targets). In a number of cases the reporting was done on the basis of 'achieved' or 'not achieved'. An example of a non-key target that was included in the planning documents, but was not reported on, is a target to establish a ratio between inspection hours and demand. The annual report also contained a number of performance measures for which no targets had been set. Examples included number of slaughtermen licensed, income generated, and number of statutory notices served.

Figure 6.1: Map of mission, objectives, targets and performance measures

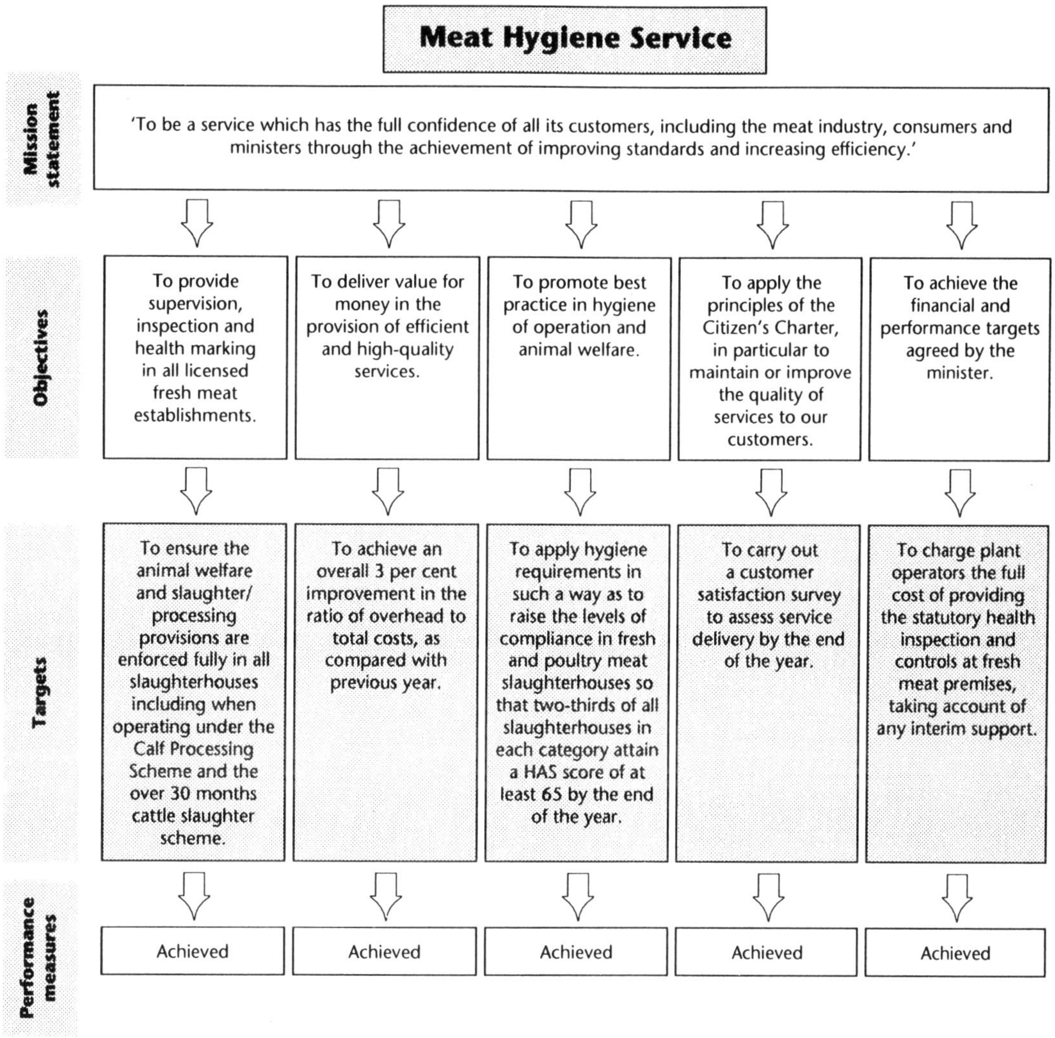

Note: the targets and performance measures above are only a selection of those contained in the corporate and business plans and annual report. Key targets are shown by shaded boxes. However, where gaps are shown (if any) this indicates that a target/performance measure was absent.

6.2.2 Driver and Vehicle Licensing (Northern Ireland)

A map of the Driver and Vehicle Licensing is given in Figure 6.2. Driver and Vehicle Licensing (Northern Ireland) was launched as an executive agency within the Department of the Environment for Northern Ireland in 1993. The agency is responsible for the licensing of drivers, the registration and licensing of vehicles and the collection and enforcement of vehicle excise duty. Its mission is to 'promote compliance with relevant legislation covering the licensing of drivers and vehicles in Northern Ireland'.

From the mission statement, two broad objectives were developed (as shown in Figure 6.2). The first of these focused on the efficiency and effectiveness of the agency, the second on the quality of customer service. Both these objectives had related key and non-key targets. All the agency's key targets could be related back to its objectives, as could four of its six non-key targets. Those that could not were work-programme targets. Within the annual report, all the agency's key targets had related performance measures. None of the non-key targets were reported in the annual report. As in the case of the Meat Hygiene Service, reporting was often on the basis of 'achieved' or 'not achieved'.

Figure 6.2: Map of mission, objectives, targets and performance measures

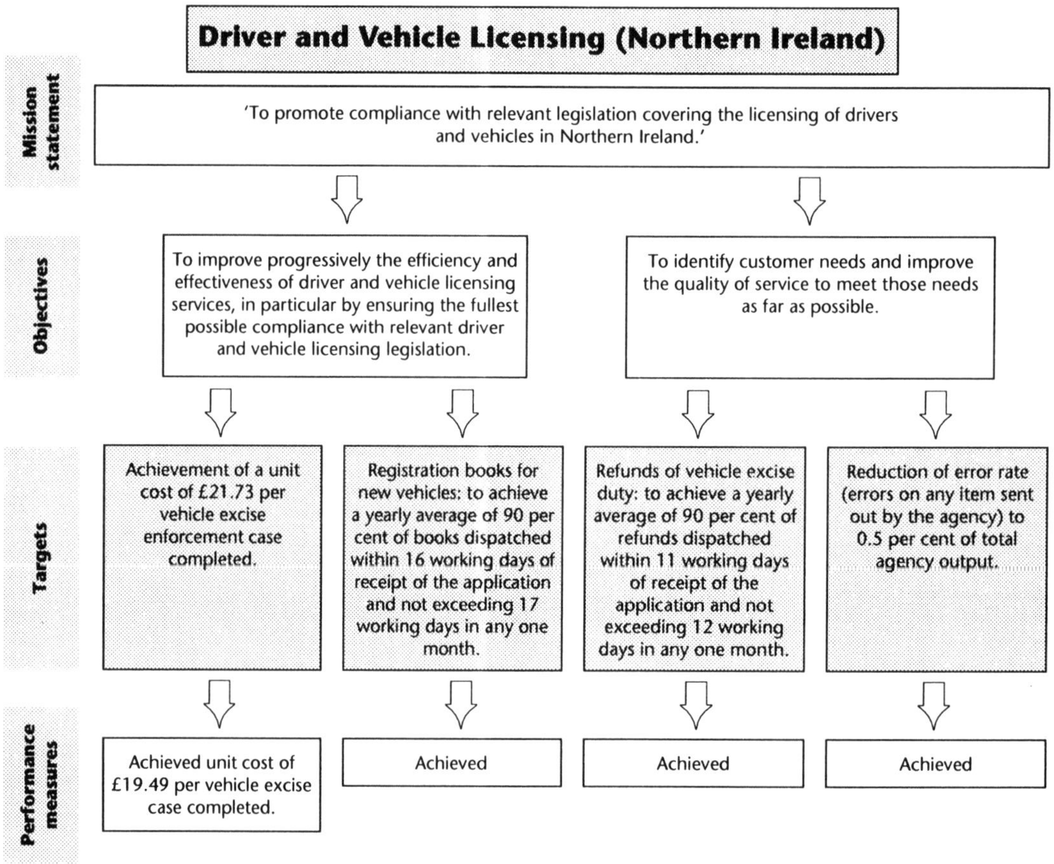

Note: the targets and performance measures above are only a selection of those contained in the corporate and business plans and annual report. Key targets are shown by shaded boxes. However, where gaps are shown (if any) this indicates that a target/performance measure was absent.

6.2.3 Defence Clothing and Textiles Agency

A map of the Defence Clothing and Textiles Agency (DCTA) is given in Figure 6.3. The DCTA was formed as an agency of the Ministry of Defence in 1994. Its activities are related to the supply of uniforms, clothing and specialist equipment to the armed forces. The agency's mission is to 'provide on behalf of the Quartermaster-General an agreed range of products and services to meet the operational requirements of the Ministry of Defence and other defined customers within agreed standards, and in the most cost-effective manner'.

The agency had five objectives (as seen in Figure 6.3), all of which had at least one key target and one non-key target related to them. In total, the agency had 19 key targets (12 of which could be related back to objectives) and 71 non-key targets (43 of which could be related back to objectives). As was fairly typical for most agencies, the unrelated targets were mostly work-programme targets. Unrelated targets included establishing and promulgating a DCTA health and safety policy, and restructuring the DCTA organisation to be based primarily on multi-disciplinary groups in parallel with collocation. Considering the large number of targets contained within the corporate and business plans, the agency highlighted a comparatively low number of performance measures in its annual report. There were performance measures for only four of the key targets (as shown in the Figure 6.3) and two of the non-key targets (not shown).

Figure 6.3: Map of mission, objectives, targets and performance measures

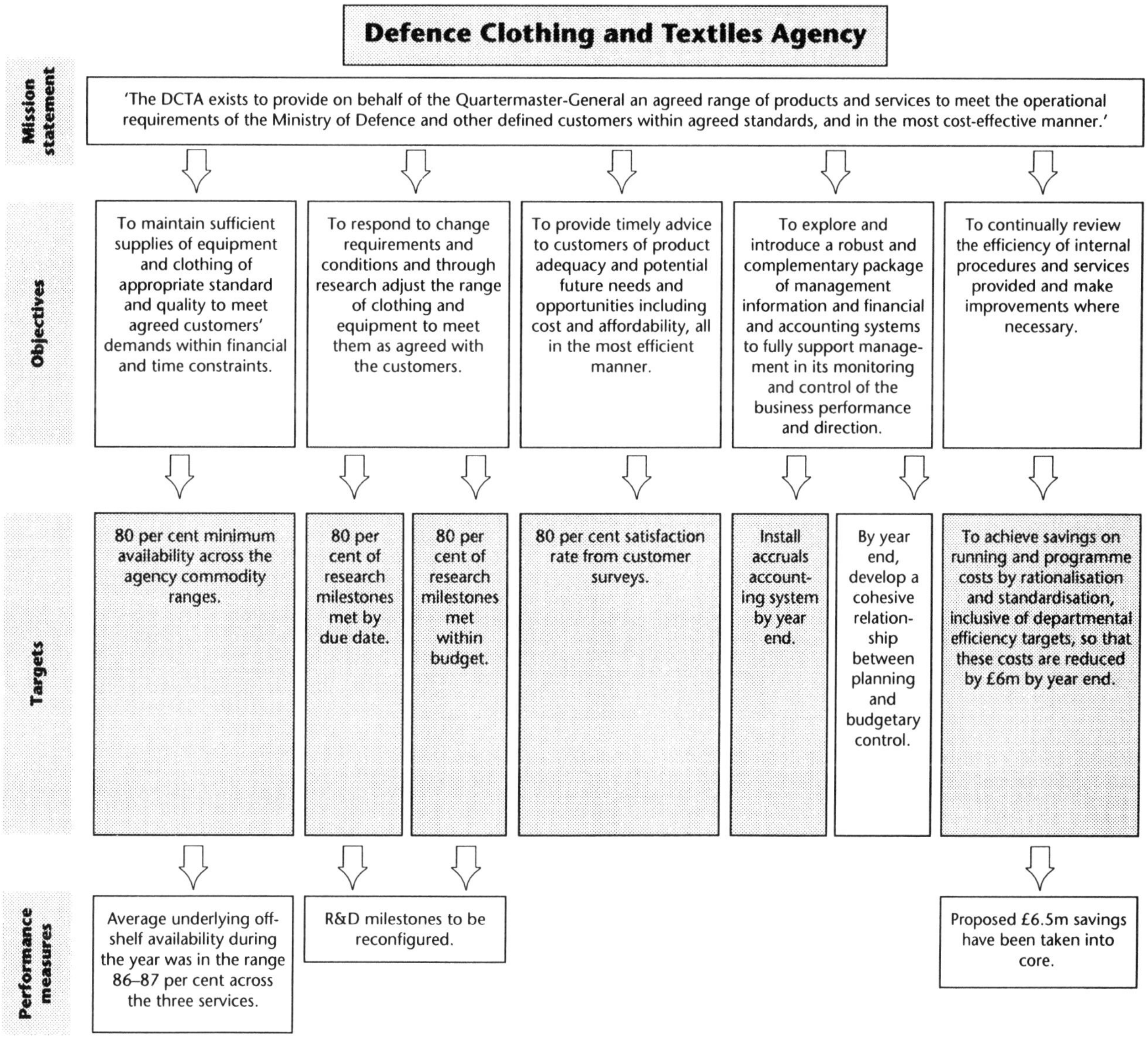

Note: the targets and performance measures above are only a selection of those contained in the corporate and business plans and annual report. Key targets are shown by shaded boxes. However, where gaps are shown (if any) this indicates that a target/performance measure was absent.

6.2.4 Public Record Office of Northern Ireland

A map of the Public Record Office of Northern Ireland (PRONI) is given in Figure 6.4. PRONI was formed as an agency of the Department of the Environment for Northern Ireland in 1995, and is responsible for identifying and preserving Northern Ireland's archival heritage and for providing access to that heritage in line with open-government standards (for full statement, see Figure 6.4).

Figure 6.4: Map of mission, objectives, targets and performance measures

Public Record Office of Northern Ireland

Mission statement: 'To identify and preserve Northern Ireland's archival heritage and to ensure public access to that heritage which fully meets open-government standards.'

Objectives	Liaise systematically with those bodies generating Northern Ireland records and potential private depositors to ensure the selection and acquisition of records of historical importance and to give particular attention to those records unique to the Northern Ireland situation.	Arrange, catalogue and index such records in an orderly and efficient manner, taking advantage – where it represents best value for money – of a modern system of information management.	Preserve all records selected for permanent preservation to the standard and in the format that gives full weight to both good archival practice and economic costs.	Co-ordinate arrangements for access to Northern Ireland public records and improve effectiveness in the release of such records by identifying all material due for sensitivity review in accordance with open-government standards.	Provide a public service that enables customers to use the records in conformity with the standards of the Citizen's Charter and improves public understanding of that part of the national heritage held by PRONI.
Targets	In April, PRONI will reorganise its staff resources according to its core function and establish a single section to progress the whole area of acquisition on a proactive basis.	To process 1,100 linear feet of privately deposited records.	Formulate, quantify and cost, by April, a preservation strategy that will embrace all the different types of records selected for permanent preservation.	PRONI will improve access facilities to the records through its systematic programme of subject indexing all open records (75 per cent by next March and 100 per cent by the following March).	By April, reduce waiting time from 60 minutes or less to 45 minutes or less in 90 per cent of cases.
Performance measures		1,306 linear feet processed.			

Note: the targets and performance measures above are only a selection of those contained in the corporate and business plans and annual report. Key targets are shown by shaded boxes. However, where gaps are shown (if any) this indicates that a target/performance measure was absent.

In pursuit of this mission, PRONI had five objectives, as illustrated in Figure 6.4. Each of these objectives had at least one related non-key target, but only the second objective had a key target related to it. The agency has a total of six key and 43 non-key targets. All the key targets were contained within the business plan; the non-key targets appeared only in the corporate plan. Only two of the six key targets could be related to an objective (that is, four out of six could not). An example of a key target that could not be related to an objective was a target to reduce the unit cost of £16.62 per reader visit by 6 per cent to £15.79 without diminishing the quality of service. Performance measures in the annual report covered all the agency's key targets (although these are not all shown in Figure 6.4) but, in common with many of the other agencies, performance measures were not reported for non-key targets.

6.2.5 Scottish Office Pensions Agency

A map of the Scottish Office Pensions Agency is given in Figure 6.5. The Scottish Office Pensions Agency became an executive agency in 1993, assuming the responsibilities previously held by the Scottish Office Superannuation Division. Its mission statement took the form of four aims, as detailed in Figure 6.5.

The agency had five objectives, four of which had related targets. No targets were given for the provision of timely and accurate information about changes to scheme policies and regulations. The agency has seven key targets, which appeared only in the business plan. There were also 36 non-key targets in the corporate and business plans. Of these, 19 could be related to the agency's objectives. The agency's performance-measurement and reporting system was reasonably thorough, with all key targets and 13 of the 15 non-key targets in the corporate plan having a related performance measure in the annual report. However, none of the non-key targets in the business plan had a related performance measure. Although the majority of these were work-programme targets, some were not, including a target relating to the proportions of late submissions paid by the due date, and a target regarding response time to enquiries.

Figure 6.5: Map of mission, objectives, targets and performance measures

Scottish Office Pensions Agency

Mission statement

'The aims of the Scottish Office Pensions Agency are as follows:
- to administer, on behalf of the Secretary of State, the public service pension, premature retirement, compensation and injury benefit schemes for which the Secretary of State has administrative responsibility so as to provide an efficient and effective service for the benefit of those who use the schemes at an economic cost to the public purse;
- to prepare in accordance with government policy the regulations governing these and other schemes for which the Secretary of State has regulatory responsibility;
- to determine questions under the regulations on which there is a right of appeal to the Secretary of State; and
- to advise the Secretary of State on occupational pensions policy generally.'

Objectives	To provide a timely, accurate and helpful service to members of the schemes administered by SOPA, and their employers, in line with the principles of the Citizen's Charter.	To collect and pay, promptly and accurately, sums due under these schemes, and to arrange for their proper accounting and budgeting.	To promulgate timely and accurately information about changes to scheme policies and regulations to local authorities and other bodies administering schemes regulated by SOPA.	To reduce over time the ratio of running costs to caseload.	To provide appropriate policy advice to ministers and departments of the Scottish Office on their pensions responsibilities generally and in order to regulate and develop the schemes for which they are responsible in accordance with government policies.
Targets	To carry out a survey to measure customer satisfaction with administration of the teachers' superannuation scheme, taking account of experience gained from the previous year's NHS survey.	To ensure that awards and transfer payments are accurate to within 1 per cent of their value in 99 per cent of cases.		Unit costs, e.g. £13.60 in cash terms, based on direct running costs.	To provide policy advice that is consistent with public service pension policy and takes account of operational objectives of Scottish Office departments, within the required timescales.
Performance measures	Customer satisfaction survey nearing completion at end of year.	Awards and transfer payments were accurate to within 1 per cent of their value in 99 per cent of cases.		Unit costs, e.g. £13.53 in cash terms, based on direct running costs.	Target met to the satisfaction of departments and ministers.

Note: the targets and performance measures above are only a selection of those contained in the corporate and business plans and annual report. Key targets are shown by shaded boxes. However, where gaps are shown (if any) this indicates that a target/performance measure was absent.

Overall, the maps presented in Figures 6.1–6.5 provide partial illustrations of the results presented in Tables 6.1–6.3. In many cases the links between key targets in the planning documents and performance measures in the annual reports were strong (key targets are represented by shaded boxes in Figures 6.1–6.5). Almost 85 per cent of key targets in the business plans had at least one performance measure in the annual reports (Table 6.2). For example, PRONI had a key target to 'process 1,100 linear feet of privately deposited records'; the performance reported in the annual report was '1,306 linear feet processed' (Figure 6.4). Similarly, the Scottish Office Pensions Agency had a key target to 'ensure that awards and transfer payments are accurate to within 1 per cent of their value in 99 per cent of cases'; the performance measurement reported in the annual report was that transfer payments were accurate to within 1 per cent of their value in 99 per cent of cases (Figure 6.5).

The majority of key targets in both planning documents are used to report on performance in the annual reports of agencies (Tables 6.1 and 6.2 show 84.7 per cent with business plans and 67.5 per cent with corporate plans). However, a significant minority of key targets are not reported in the annual reports. This is seen in the map of the Defence Clothing and Textiles Agency (Figure 6.3), where key targets relating to customer satisfaction and the installation of an accruals accounting system are not reported. Furthermore, key targets relating to research milestones (in terms of meeting them and keeping within budget) were not specifically reported, but rather an explanation was given that they would have to be 'reconfigured'.

With respect to non-key targets (those not shaded in Figures 6.1–6.5), the maps indicate substantial non-linkage between targets set in the planning documents and performance measures used in the annual reports (non-key targets are seldom used as a basis for reporting through the medium of the annual report). For example, PRONI had a non-key target relating to formulating, quantifying and costing a preservation strategy; no performance measure relating to this was reported in the annual report. Similarly, a non-key target concerned with reducing waiting time was not reported in the annual report (for these examples, see Figure 6.4). Only about 10 per cent of non-key targets included in the business plans of agencies were reported in the annual reports (Table 6.2).

6.3 Analysis and discussion

It has been argued previously that an agency has a responsibility to account to those outside its management, and that the annual report is an important medium in this process. It is further argued that, although the information contained in traditional financial statements may be important, in the majority of cases wider performance information is critical in adequately discharging the accountability of agencies. The importance of agencies measuring and reporting on performance has been recognised in a number of NSI publications. Performance, rather than spending, has been emphasised, and it is argued that such a shift of attention will lead to a more accountable public sector, and provide a stimulus for better management and performance improvement.

It was suggested in Chapter 3 that whereas a lack of disclosure may suit some managers, the external pressure provided by the provision of information externally encourages a focus for the organisation. This can then provide a catalyst for managers as they seek to improve performance and makes the possibility of ineffective or illegitimate actions less likely. A strong demand for the discharge of accountability might encourage the development of a clearly articulated planning and control framework. Moreover, the relationship between the planning system and the discharge of accountability is further highlighted when it is argued that objectives and targets can provide a platform for the discharge of accountability.

The results in this research provide evidence that the targets contained in the planning documents provide a basis for the reporting of performance through the mechanism of the annual report. Twenty-four agencies were analysed to identify the linkages between the targets included in the planning documents and the reporting of performance in the annual reports. Although there are far fewer performance measures in the annual reports than targets in the planning documents, the majority of performance measures are related to targets in the planning documents (63.7 per cent of performance measures could be related to targets in the business plans). A system of targeting and then reporting against targets (as suggested in HM Treasury, 1992) is apparent. However, the majority of targets are not reported in the annual reports. Doing otherwise could result in significant information overload, given, for example, that there were 939 targets in the 24 business plans alone.

It is also clear that it is the key targets of agencies that provide the platform for reporting. Over 84 per cent of key targets in the business plans had at least one related performance measure in the annual reports (67.5 per cent relating to corporate plans). With reference to non-key targets the percentage was less than 15 per cent in both types of planning document. Furthermore, over 76 per cent of performance measures were related to a key target in both types of planning document, even though only 32 per cent of all targets were key targets (437 out of 1,362). Given that the key targets are generally the high-level targets and cover critical success areas, it would seem that such a form of reporting would be appropriate to external users. This would also be in accord with guidance given by HM Treasury (1992).

Notwithstanding the above, it is perhaps surprising that so many of the performance measures used in the annual reports could not be related to targets. The method that was employed ensured that 24 matched sets of documents (business plan, corporate plan and annual report) were used relating to the same time period for each agency. Over 36 per cent (160 out of 441) of the performance measures used in the annual report were not related to targets in the business plans. With reference to the corporate plans, the figure was much higher with 67.3 per cent (297 out of 441) unrelated to a target.

The potential danger is that an aspect of performance is being measured (and being valued) that is unrelated to a target, unrelated to an objective and unrelated to the overall mission of the agency. By measuring it, there is the potential of giving it value that encourages the production of, for example, more of it or an improved quality relating to it. Yet, if the aspect of performance is unrelated to targets, objectives and mission, then such focus can be extremely wasteful. This is not necessarily the case, however, as the results may merely denote that the targets have been inappropriately developed and need to be revisited. Nevertheless, it indicates a degree of confusion that would appear to undermine the focus of the organisation. For example, in the case of the Meat Hygiene Service, should the number of slaughtermen licensed, the income generated or the number of statutory notices served (all performance measures reported in the annual report of the agency although no targets are included in the planning documents – see the discussion relating to Figure 6.3) be targeted? Are they important? Do they relate to the furthering of the overall mission?

Another important issue relating to the publication of performance information, although not central to the issues being explored here, is that of the reliability of externally reported performance information. If no verification of the performance numbers reported by an agency is required, then there may be a temptation to exaggerate performance. Given that external parties may use externally reported performance information to make judgements and decisions regarding an agency, then the case for some degree of independent verification appears to be strong. Although cost–benefit issues need to be considered, the increasing emphasis placed by HM Treasury on externally reporting performance information (see, for example, HM Government, 1995) would appear to provide a *prima facie* case for some degree of verification. It should be noted that almost all the performance information analysed in this study had not been subject to independent verification, as is the case with performance information reported by the vast majority of UK public-sector organisations. A Public Accounts Committee report (1997, p. vii) recommended that the Treasury should aim to achieve 'independent validation'. A fuller discussion of this issue is contained in Likierman (1997).

7

The Views of Agency Chief Executives in Northern Ireland

The previous two chapters identified the ways in which the mission statements, objectives and targets in the planning documents of UK agencies were co-ordinated, or linked, and the extent to which performance information contained in the annual reports of agencies was consistent with the targets. Overall, although weaknesses were identified, they provided evidence of reasonably co-ordinated systems of objectives and targets, and the widespread use of targets, especially key targets, in reporting on performance through the medium of the annual report. In an attempt to explore these issues further, a series of interviews was conducted with the chief executives of nine Northern Ireland agencies. The results of these interviews are presented in this chapter. A detailed method relating to this part of the research was presented in section 4.3.

7.1 The Next Steps Initiative and Northern Ireland

As outlined previously, the impact of the NSI has been considerable. In Great Britain, following the launch of the programme in 1988, three agencies had been established by the end of that year and by the end of 1998 113 agencies were operating. Northern Ireland was slower to respond, although here too the impact has been significant. The first agency was created in 1990, and by the end of 1998 25 agencies were in existence.

The Northern Ireland civil service (NICS) is separate from the British civil service. It is, as Birrell (1978, p. 305) has described, 'a unique example of a regional civil service within the UK civil service ... and provides the administrative machinery for the province'. Although the NICS does not necessarily have to replicate all civil service reforms introduced in Great Britain, it is custom and practice for general policies to be largely followed (Loughlin, 1992). The reforms did not initially extend to Northern Ireland and, as Knox and McHugh (1990) suggest, the NICS, though not pressing to be excluded from the reform, did not rush to implement its recommendations. However, over time, the agency model was embraced, albeit in a lagged fashion, by the NICS. Knox and McHugh (p. 266) argue that the Northern Ireland approach to NSI has been 'studiously progressive, learning from the British experience but cognisant of the specific circumstances of size and political sensitivities'.

Northern Ireland has a population of 1.6 million. The NICS has some 30,000 civil servants, approximately equalling a medium-sized department in Whitehall. Prior to the creation of a devolved Assembly in 1999 as part of the implementation of the Belfast Agreement, the NICS consisted of six government departments and the Northern Ireland Office. The first Northern Ireland agency was established in April 1990 (the Training and Employment Agency), with two more following in 1991. This number increased gradually, accelerated in 1996 when ten agencies were added, and by December 1998 had grown to 25 agencies. Eleven of these came from a single department (the Department of the Environment). At this time, these 25 agencies employed over 19,000 civil servants. On average, a Northern Ireland agency had 771 civil servants, and 14 of the 25 agencies (56 per cent of the total) had fewer than 300 civil servants. By contrast, the average size of a British agency was approximately 2,500, with only 37 out of 113 British agencies (33 per cent) having fewer than 300 civil servants. Overall, 138 agencies were in existence throughout the UK (Northern Ireland and Great Britain), with over 377,000 civil servants (76 per cent of all civil servants) working in such organisations.

7.2 Results

A semi-structured interview approach was used to gauge the perceptions of the nine chief executives, and questions were asked relating to the executives' background and awareness, changes since agencification, the use and importance of targets, and the benefits and drawbacks of a rational approach with its emphasis on quantification. The interview guide used is shown in the Appendix.

7.2.1 Background and awareness of chief executives

A number of questions were asked to establish such factors as the length of service in the organisation (of function), awareness of terms such as 'objectives' and 'targets', perceptions with respect to the difference between the terms 'key target' and 'other (non-key) target', and degree of involvement in the development of mission statements, objectives, targets and performance measures (see Appendix, questions 1–4). Possibly the longer the period the individual has worked in the organisation (or function) the greater the likelihood of a reasonable level of understanding of the agency's management processes. This can also be used to establish whether the individual worked for the organisation (in the function) before agencification. The chief executives were questioned on the awareness of terms so that the terminology being used by the researchers in subsequent questions could be explained, thus avoiding possible misunderstanding.

Four of the respondents had worked in the same function (which was now an agency) before and after agencification. The other five chief executives joined their agencies after they had been set up. Previously, they had all worked in other parts of the public sector. Their periods of service in their present agencies (including service in the same function before agencification) ranged from 31 years to one year. It was clear, from both questioning and discussion, that they were all well aware of the terms 'mission statements', 'objectives', 'targets' and 'performance measures'. However, perceptions with respect to the difference between the terms 'key target' and 'other (non-key) target' were varied, with four of the chief executives restricting the use of the term 'key target' to ministers' targets, Charter Mark targets or Citizen's Charter targets. The other agencies tended to use the term to reflect all targets that were published or targets that were categorised as 'key' by the agency itself. One agency used the term 'priority target' rather than 'key target', although the general import of the term was identical.

With respect to their degree of involvement, either directly or indirectly, in the development of mission statements, objectives, targets and performance measures in the agency, all the chief executives described themselves as being 'very involved'. Typical of the comments made as they expanded on this were:

- *My involvement is central to the process.*
- *I am responsible for drafting the corporate plans and business plans. A co-ordinating or 'cajoling' role...greatly involved in setting objectives and targets.*

7.2.2 Changed focus since agencification and process of developing mission statement, objectives and targets

Questions 5–11 (see Appendix) focused on the process by which mission statements, objectives, targets and performance measures are developed and the extent to which the importance of such has changed since agencification. As discussed earlier, the NSI emphasises the significance of mission statements, objectives and targets and the need for these to be co-ordinated. Furthermore, it has been argued in a number of NSI-related publications that targets should reflect the concerns of all stakeholders and be 'stretching'.

With respect to the extent to which the importance of mission statements, objectives, targets and performance measures had changed since agencification, there appeared to be two distinct types of response. Five chief executives indicated that the change was not dramatic because the agency had been on this road prior to agencification, sometimes as a result of other (largely complementary) initiatives. However, each of these agencies indicated that the process had been honed and intensified since (or perhaps because of) agencification. Examples of statements made by chief executives in this group were:

- *Before we became an agency we were not into measurement to the same extent but always had a culture of serving the public. There was a culture change – complete process re-engineering started in 1990, leading to an integrated computer system and the necessity for quantification and precise specification of data and terms. Executive agency status fitted into the new mental attitude.*
- *In general very little has changed, but we have become more focused and refined. Terms such as 'objectives' and 'targets' were used before becoming an agency, but these were not published or reported to the minister. This was due to the nature of the business [a complex, integrated organisation which must be controlled and managed] and was always part of the organisation's culture, although to a lesser extent prior to agency status.*

The other four respondents saw the impact of agencification as being more pronounced and bringing about a major change in focus and management. Typical of observations made by these chief executives were:

- *Agency status has been a great success.... Every member of staff receives a copy of the corporate plan and business plan. From this a forward job plan is produced for each member of staff containing performance targets – every performance target should be contained within someone's job plan. Everything now focuses on producing the results according to our key performance targets.*
- *The agency has become target focused and these targets relate directly to customer service. Some are measured on a daily basis to assist in the deployment of staff. There has gradually been a tightening of targets and the staff have become more conscious of them.*

A number of questions were asked to identify the way in which mission statements, objectives and targets were developed, and the influence of various stakeholders in such processes. As discussed earlier, a rigid rational management approach suggests a largely top-down process where mission is developed prior to drafting objectives and targets. Karbhari and Pendlebury's (1997) research has provided some evidence of a more flexible approach.

Two main approaches were identified regarding the way in which the mission statement was developed. Five of the nine chief executives interviewed described a process that involved both 'internal' (for example, the parent department and the agency) and 'external' parties (for example, 'customers' or a consultative group). The degree of involvement of each of these groups varied. With reference to the other four agencies, a process that relied much more heavily on the parent department and the agency was described, with little reference to other parties. In all nine cases the influence of the agency itself was viewed as dominant. The importance of the 'Fraser figure'[8] in the parent department was mentioned on a number of occasions as being a welcome and useful point of contact.

Respondents were asked to explain the order in which mission statements, objectives and targets were developed. From the rational management literature, a sequential process commencing with the formulation of a mission statement and then proceeding to objectives and targets is typical. In seven of the nine agencies this sequence was described, with varying terms used. However, it was clear that in none of these instances was the sequencing rigid, and in most cases the chief executive viewed the process as being iterative. Examples of comments relating to this are:

- *Mission statement, objectives and targets in that order.... There may have been a little reverse tweaking.*
- *It was an iterative process which developed an internal momentum as the mindset of the organisation changed. It was a process of refinement involving staff, directors and managers in a process which they could identify with, commit to and deliver against. The agency began with aspirations which were refined into objectives and then key targets.*
- *All were developed at approximately the same time but in the order aims, objectives and then targets.... However, some of the targets have led to the objectives and the aims being revisited.*

In the two other cases, a more bottom-up approach was described. Here the focus was initially lower down in the organisation (at division or core-activity level) and then built up to objectives and mission. In one case it was stated that the targets were considered prior to the formulation of the mission and objectives, whereas in the other the initial focus was on core activities prior to the formulation of mission statement and objectives. As in the other seven agencies, the interviewers developed an impression of a fairly flexible and iterative approach.

Questions were asked regarding whether all objectives would have targets and whether targets could be set that were unrelated to objectives. With a strict interpretation of the rational management model, one would expect all objectives to have targets and all targets to be capable of being linked to objectives. The evidence from the interviews suggested that the majority of chief executives perceived problems in identifying targets for all objectives, although it was often stated that attempts were made to measure where measurement was possible and appropriate. Some comments regarding the possibility that certain objectives may have no targets were:

- *Sometimes it is difficult to measure success in as specific a way as the textbook would suggest. There are some very important objectives which are difficult to measure.*
- *It is possible, but quantified targets are developed wherever possible.*
- *Targets have been established for most areas but the third aim [the agency's advisory role] is more difficult to measure.*
- *It is possible due to the disparate nature of the work.*

In some cases it was noted that, even if there is no published target relating to a particular objective, there may be 'internal targets' (presumably not included in the corporate and business plans). Very little evidence was provided of a deliberate attempt formally to establish or review linkages between objectives and targets, although most chief executives were of the opinion that these links were fairly strong. With regard to the possibility of a target being developed that was unrelated to an objective, the vast majority of chief executives perceived that this would not happen because of the review process regarding targets (although no deliberate attempt formally to review the links between objectives and targets was described). However, one chief executive highlighted the fact that 'milestone' targets may not be able to be related to any particular objective but rather supported the 'overall business structure and objectives'. Another chief executive acknowledged that having a target that was not related to an objective was 'not impossible because they are not linked as a conscious effort'.

A related question dealt with whether important aspects of the agency's performance were not capable of being captured within objectives and targets, and measured through quantitative performance measures (see Appendix, question 10). Seven of the chief executives perceived that all important aspects of the agency could be captured within such a taxonomy, although three qualified this with respect to advisory and policy issues (particularly relating to the role of the chief executive). Furthermore, a few specifically mentioned that, although difficulties had existed earlier with reference to this issue, these had been overcome. Two of the chief executives explained that, although most important aspects of performance had targets and performance measures, possibly this was not the case with all areas. Specific comments relating to this were:

- *It is such a big business that it is bound to be difficult to measure everything.*
- *Independence and objectivity, which are cornerstones of the service provided, are difficult to fit into this scheme. These areas are judged rather than measured.*

A question relating to the extent to which targets were 'stretching' was asked. A common theme in the NSI literature is that targets should be set at levels above previous years' performance (for example, HM Government, 1997). All the chief executives were of the opinion that there was always an attempt to provide stretching targets for their agency and there has never, to their knowledge, been any bid to set easy targets in order to demonstrate 'success'. Many provided impressive examples, with the same dimension of performance, of targets becoming much tighter over time and actual performance moving in the same direction as the target (on the face of it, suggesting significantly improving performance). The use of GB benchmarks (in the case of some agencies), ministerial advisory boards, Fraser figures and parent department scrutinies were all identified as influences encouraging the setting of demanding targets. The idea that the culture in the agency was such that stretching targets were the norm was mentioned by a number of respondents. It was also suggested that too much success in meeting targets might indicate a lack of ambition in setting the targets at high-enough levels. Comments regarding this latter point were:

- *The agency accepts the discipline that a good target is one which there is a 70 per cent chance of achieving. The agency's corporate personality is one of discipline.*
- *Sometimes we fail to achieve our targets... I would be suspicious of any agency which always meets its targets.*

7.2.3 Use of targets within the agency and in reporting to the parent department

Questions 12–14 (see Appendix) attempted to establish the ways in which targets were used within the agency as part of the feedback control process and their use in reporting to the parent department. Moreover, the perceived consequences of missing targets were explored. As discussed previously, the NSI literature articulates the importance of both feedback control (utilising performance targets) within the agency (an aspect of improving managerial information as the basis for improving performance), and the need to report to the parent department (an aspect of accountability and hands-off control mechanisms). The probing of the consequences of missing targets will provide some evidence of the existence or not of a 'target-constrained' type of management environment (with potential adverse effects).

With regard to the way in which targets were used within the agency as part of the feedback control process, all the chief executives emphasised the importance of such mechanisms in reporting to the management board (if one existed), to senior managers and to employees. The enthusiasm with which a number of the chief executives explained their particular procedures was notable, and a variety of reports and charts were produced to illustrate their explanations. The overwhelming impression gained by the researchers was that this use of targets was viewed by the chief executives as extremely valuable in communicating to individuals, gaining commitment to the mission and improving the focus of individual teams within the organisation. These reasons were all perceived as important in improving management within the agency. All the agencies used monthly, or four-weekly, reporting periods, although it was noted in a few cases that it was difficult, because of management information system problems, to have exact actual performance figures each month. Typical of the comments made were:

- *Actual performance is reviewed at monthly management board meetings. Data is also collected on a weekly basis and used daily by operational managers and supervisors to make decisions on staffing etc.... Reports which compare actual performance with targets are very actively used management tools in this organisation.*
- *We operate a very structured process where individual units report to their unit manager on a very wide range of measures. A certain proportion of these measures are reported from the unit manager to the operations director. A proportion of these are then reported to the chief executive and management board. This happens monthly for quantifiable targets and quarterly for milestone targets.*
- *Performance is measured against targets on a monthly basis and copies of the performance charts are sent to all branches.... There are senior management team and team leader meetings monthly, the minutes of which are circulated, which review this information.*

With regard to reporting on achievement of targets to the parent department, generally all agencies routinely reported on a quarterly basis. This may have been to the minister, or a group in the parent department with an overseeing responsibility for the agency or to the Fraser figure. Representative of the comments made were:

- *The agency reports quarterly to the ministerial advisory board, submitting a performance statement containing key targets, actual performance, business volume and expenditure.*
- *We report... once a quarter. A major part of this report is progress on targets.*

When questioned about the consequences, within the agency and in respect of the parent department, of missing targets, all the chief executives described fairly flexible approaches, albeit to differing degrees. There was little evidence of a widespread target-constrained style of evaluation by the agency on its employees, nor by the parent departments on their agencies. However, one chief executive highlighted the case that with some requirements of the parent department (the keeping within financial budget and the introduction of policy initiatives) there was no room for failure. Many of the chief executives distinguished between failure through lack of performance (that would not be tolerated) and failure through changed circumstances or unrealistically optimistic targets (that would be tolerated). Evidence of the opportunity to discuss and explain any missed targets was provided. In two agencies, reference to staff bonus implications of missed targets was made. In these cases, it was stated that a bonus might be paid even if targets were missed but a reasonable and acceptable explanation was provided. Examples of comments made were:

- *If it is realised that targets were not attainable, or if the resource position has changed, then that is taken into account. However, if the target is missed because individuals are not doing their jobs, then that has serious repercussions.... The chief executive is ... answerable to the minister who challenges when targets are missed. However, the minister is reasonable and takes explanations into account.... The system will accommodate unforeseens – it will not accommodate failure because of lack of performance.*
- *Within the agency there are recriminations if targets are missed through negligence. There is no difficulty reporting failure if events have conspired to make achievement of the target impossible.... The department doesn't seem too concerned if targets are missed – they seem to take a mature attitude, recognising that the targets are challenging.*
- *We live in the real world and we don't expect the offices to meet all their targets.... It doesn't take much to knock a particular district out.... If the agency doesn't meet its overall targets then they get a rap on the knuckles from the minister unless there is a good story to tell. There would be more of a comeback if targets were missed consistently.*

7.2.4 Importance of different types of targets

HM Treasury (1992) recommended that targets be developed under four main headings: financial targets (for example, live within budget, sales revenue generated); volume (for example, number of cases handled); efficiency (for example, cost per vehicle tested, cases handled per employee); and quality (for example, waiting time, error rate). It was argued that in most cases it would be appropriate for each agency to develop some targets under each heading. Furthermore, it was suggested that such targets can provide an important aspect of the reporting of performance through the medium of the annual report (as discussed in detail in Chapter 6). However, Hyndman and Anderson (1998) have suggested that different groups attach varying levels of importance to different types of targets. Questions were asked (see Appendix, questions 15 and 16) regarding the importance of different types of targets (from the agency management perspective, the parent department's perspective, and the public's or customers' perspective) and the use of such targets in external reporting.

With reference to the importance of different types of targets to different stakeholders, clear patterns emerged. In eight of the nine agencies the chief executive perceived quality targets as the most important type of target from a customer/public perspective. In one of these eight cases it was perceived as being of equal importance to price (where the agency was charging for the service). With regard to the parent department, chief executives perceived financial issues (often keeping within budget) as the most important (with seven of the agencies stating that these were the most important or equal most important), although other types of targets were mentioned as important. In two of these cases the financial targets were viewed as constraints within which the agency had to operate. The most frequent reply regarding the importance to the agency itself was that all targets were important (five respondents). An explanation of the interrelationships between the various target types was frequently offered, for example, higher volume allowed unit costs to be reduced. In one case it was admitted that, because the parent department viewed certain financial targets as essential, it was inevitable that the agency would prioritise the same targets. Examples of statements made by the chief executives were:

Perceived importance to parent department

- *The budget target is overriding, but it may be renegotiated if exceptional circumstances make this necessary.*
- *They are only really worried if the financial target is missed. If you overspent it would be a horrendous crime.*
- *The financial target is a constraint – the agency cannot spend more money than it has been allocated.*

Perceived importance to customer/public

- *Quality of service is the most important, particularly time taken.*
- *Quality is of paramount importance to the public.*

Perceived importance to the agency

- *All are important and interlinked – quality and efficiency within a properly run organisation lead into financial returns.*
- *They are interrelated and therefore cannot be put into a hierarchy.*

All the chief executives stated that targets were used as a basis for reporting in annual reports, although several highlighted the fact that generally only performance against key targets was reported. Three of the nine chief executives, although acknowledging the use of targets in this manner, suggested that the external readership of the annual report was limited. One of the chief executives recognised the accountability function of such reporting, but viewed the annual report more in terms of a public relations document. Typical comments in respect of the external reporting of performance against targets were:

- *Mainly we report our performance against key targets in our annual report.*
- *Transparency is very important. Publishing performance against targets is an aspect of this.*
- *Key targets and general detail on the Citizen's Charter targets are published in the annual report ... people do not read it* [the report] *but it requires a lot of effort to produce.*
- *I don't think our annual report is avidly read by anybody. It is more a PR and publicity document than an accountability document.... However, it fulfils the accountability function and should be an accountability document.*

7.2.5 The perceived benefits of the rational approach with its emphasis on quantification

Questions were asked to identify the perceived benefits of an approach that emphasises mission statement, objectives, targets and performance measures and whether, overall, it has led to an improvement in performance (see Appendix, questions 17–19). The overall objective of the NSI is to deliver better-quality central-government services for the benefit of taxpayers, customers and staff (*Next Steps Briefing Note,* 1996). Question 19 specifically focused on whether such a rational approach had achieved this objective. In addition, the perceptions of the twin objectives of improving management and providing greater accountability (as identified by HM Treasury, 1992) were explored.

Overwhelmingly, the most frequently expressed benefit was related to the sense of focus that such an approach provided. This was sometimes referred to in terms of purpose or direction and was highlighted in all nine agencies. A number of chief executives expanded at length and with enthusiasm regarding this perceived improvement. Other benefits mentioned included the provision of a means of control, the visibility that the approach gives thus enabling a more questioning approach to be adopted, the opportunity to rethink the structure of the service and relate it to objectives and targets, and the ability of individuals and units to identify more directly with the activities in the agency. Typical comments were:

- *The agency knows exactly what it has got to achieve – overall, in divisions and lower down ...* [having targets] *sets a sense of purpose, direction, pride and achievement ...* [and] *provides a control mechanism.*
- *Targeting and measuring what has to be done gives a structure... The functional split led to creative friction, which has been very positive. Now the focus is on customers and measurement... Target-setting and measurement enters the bloodstream – individuals who never talked about targets at all just talk about them quite naturally now; it is accepted.... Measurement leads to a sense of achievement.*
- *It gives people inside the organisation a greater sense of direction and therefore achievement. It also ensures a better service to the clients/customers/stakeholders.*

The majority of chief executives perceived the twin objectives of improving management and providing greater accountability as equally important, with five of the nine respondents suggesting this. A natural linkage between improving management and greater accountability was identified by these chief executives. One commented, 'Both are important ... management and accountability are indivisible.' Of the remaining four, they were equally split regarding the paramountcy of improving management and greater accountability. In each of these cases the important linkage with the other objective was acknowledged. For example, a well-developed and co-ordinated set of objectives and targets to facilitate better management (which was viewed as of primary importance) was seen as providing a good basis for the discharge of accountability.

All the respondents perceived that focusing on mission, objectives, targets and performance measures had improved the performance of the agency for all stakeholders. It was argued that the agency management, the sponsoring department (or minister) and the customer or general public were each benefiting. One of the respondents was of the opinion that perhaps the customer (or general public) was unaware of any improvement or the extent of the improvement. As in the case of responses to question 11 (see Appendix) regarding the degree of 'stretch', impressive examples were provided of how performance had improved over time since agencification. However, one chief executive suggested that performance would have improved anyway in his agency (due to changed working practices and improvements in technology), although perhaps not to the same extent. Examples of customer surveys and procedures for monitoring and dealing with customer complaints were provided as evidence of improving performance from a customer perspective, and various statements were made to highlight increasing satisfaction from a sponsoring department's perspective. Examples of various comments made were:

- *Without question performance has improved ... from everyone's point of view, particularly the government and the public.*
- *Without a doubt, from everybody's point of view, performance is improving.... The department was very impressed with the agency plans – gobsmacked.... A customer survey also showed that customers were fairly contented.*
- *We can demonstrate improvement to customers (although customer demands may run ahead of this).... Attitudes within the organisation have changed – staff have become much more customer-focused, not just setting targets for the sake of it. It's now, 'We're civil servants – we're here to serve the public' not, 'I'm a civil servant, I'm here to have a job' which was an attitude prevalent in the past.... We can demonstrate to the department that service has improved.*

7.2.6 The perceived drawbacks of the rational approach with its emphasis on quantification

The rational approach, with its emphasis on quantification and clear means–ends relationships, is not without problems. It has been suggested that the application of such ideas to complex organisations is problematical. For example, McSweeney (1988), in discussing value-for-money audits and the role of the Audit Commission, examines a number of the difficulties of such an approach. These include the lack of a direct and knowable link between intentions and outcomes, the difficulty of identifying explicit and quantifiable objectives, the ability to manipulate information, and a concentration on quantification with a resulting lack of regard for qualitative factors. Moreover, Thompson (1995) and Sharifi and Bovaird (1995) have suggested that if such systems are imposed on organisations, the organisational response may be little more than 'ritualistic' with no real commitment to the cause. Questions 20–22 (see Appendix) were used to explore these issues and identify the extent of chief executives' perceptions of drawbacks.

Although three of the chief executives considered that there were no drawbacks from a management approach that emphasises mission, objectives, targets and performance measures, the other six respondents identified a number of problems. Even though a range of different terms was used, the two most frequently identified issues related to the poor implementation of the system originally (mentioned four times) and the tendency to overemphasise numbers at the expense of judgement (mentioned three times). With reference to the first of these, two respondents mentioned that, once implemented, there was a need to 'learn' and change the system to make it more appropriate. Regarding the overemphasis on numbers, chief executives highlighted such matters as a skewed focus and a tendency to 'dehumanise' the organisation. In these cases, the need to manage the situation so as to avoid adverse consequences was stressed. Examples of comments made were:

- *We have had no drawbacks – it has worked well and will work well for organisations which are producing some form of quantifiable output.*
- *The whole thing was handled quite ham-fistedly early on in my view, in relation to efficiency.... The process was right but it was handled in a dogmatic way.*
- *There is a danger that if your mission statement, aims, objectives and targets are not well thought out and well aligned then the thing is skewed and something is neglected that shouldn't be neglected.... When this happens there is a need to review in a holistic way.*
- *There is a potential for key targets to take on a life of their own, they may be concentrated on at the expense of others. This was a problem in the early stages but there has been a deliberate change to encourage staff to regard all the supporting targets as important. Some key targets were subtly changed to link in some of the operational targets.*
- *There is the danger that the human aspect may be overlooked if there is too great a focus on targets.*

Related to the above was the question of whether the pursuit of targets could lead to inappropriate decisions or behaviour in the agency (see Appendix, question 21). The majority of chief executives (six) identified potentially inappropriate behaviour from a focusing on targets, but the general sense gained by the interviewers was that if this arose the focus would be adjusted. Four of the respondents identified particular tensions between such factors as speed and quality, or long term and short term. Yet throughout the interviews the impression was given of a flexible approach, with management managing the situation as information became available. Examples of this were:

- *It could be argued that inappropriate behaviour occurred as a result of speed targets – it was perhaps inevitable that quality would suffer in the medium term.... Once this was realised by management we tried to move from speed to quality targets.... But it was a 'difficult ship to turn around' once the speed culture had been established, even though the staff knew that the speed culture didn't make sense.*
- *Sometimes calculated risks may be required to ensure achievement of targets.... At certain times of year, the standard 1 in 10 check may be reduced to 1 in 50 to ensure that timeliness targets are met.*

The final question (see Appendix) related to whether the organisational response to systems that emphasise mission statements, objectives, targets and performance measures may be 'ritualistic'. All the respondents stated that this was not the case, although one acknowledged that at the lower levels in the organisation there was potential for this. Another stated that there was the possibility of this in the early days of such systems but that 'after a certain phase, a real commitment takes over and the focus moves towards customers'.

7.3 Analysis and discussion of results

This part of the research represents a case study of nine Northern Ireland agencies within the wider UK agency sector. Perceptions of chief executives of these agencies were identified with respect to the development, use and impact of mission statements, objectives, targets and performance measures. Chief executives were chosen because of their seniority, assumed detailed knowledge of the issues, and their ability to provide an overview of the entire operation of the agency. It is acknowledged that the views of other important stakeholders (such as customers and parent departments) would be valuable, although, because of the constraints of access, time and finance, these were not sought. Confidentiality was respected and the results are reported in a way in which specific statements cannot be attributed to particular individuals. The nine chosen from the 24 agencies covered in the earlier parts of the research were self-selecting on the basis of being reasonably accessible to the researchers and were all located in Northern Ireland. The nine are therefore not necessarily representative of all 24 agencies.

The interviews provide additional evidence that a neat sequential model, as typified by the rational management approach, is not generally used in the management of agencies. An amount of rationality exists (as evidenced by conventional planning documents and processes, and formalised targets), though a fair degree of flexibility is evidenced. For example, the order in which mission statements, objectives and targets are developed is often iterative, with a degree of 'tweaking' and 'revisiting'. A need for judgement to evaluate certain aspects of performance was highlighted. The way in which feedback is used by the senior management of the agency and by representatives of the parent department is fluid, with there being 'no difficulty reporting failure if events have conspired to make achievement of the target impossible' and departments 'taking a mature attitude, recognising that the targets are challenging'. Objectives and targets are not imposed by the parent department, but rather negotiated with the agency, often taking into account the concerns of other stakeholders. All this suggests that there is no 'one size fits all' rigid rational management model that is applied to all agencies. Where differences were found, they tended to be associated with the degree and nature of the flexibility.

The interviews provided evidence of fairly flexible controls from the centre in many respects. However, regarding financial controls, it was clear that these were tight, reflecting the fact that in the NICS the Department of Finance and Personnel (DFP) keeps a firm control on budgets, pay and personnel. It may be the case that these controls are tighter in Northern Ireland than in Great Britain, possibly caused by the smaller scale in Northern Ireland. When considering differences between the British civil service and the NICS, it has been suggested (DFP, 1984, p. 7) that these may 'stem mainly from the smaller size of the NICS and the advantages of centralising certain functions'. Yet the conclusions of Karbhari and Pendlebury (1997), in their research relating to British agencies, found a similar pattern. Although financial controls from the centre were fairly tight, they found a participative approach to the management of agencies and managers with much more freedom to control their activities since agencification.

Overall, systems more akin to what Quinn (1980) describes as logical incrementalism were described by the chief executives. In such models it is realised that not all options can be identified and analysed (as suggested by rational management models). Rather, decisions emerge through a constant process of analysis, reanalysis and modification throughout the development and implementation of a strategy in order to keep in line with the environment. It is the deliberate development of strategy by 'learning through doing'. This concept was particularly evident with respect to replies to question 5 (see Appendix) regarding the importance of mission statements, objectives, targets and performance measures since agencification. A number of respondents highlighted the evolving nature of the systems and targets as learning took place.

The respondents perceived that the importance of mission statements, objectives, targets and performance measures had changed since agencification, although to varying extents in different agencies. Overall, there was the distinct impression that this had brought significant benefits, with the sense of increased focus being the most frequently quoted. Furthermore, all the chief executives believed that this had resulted in benefits to the agency itself, the parent department and the customer. Again, these findings are in line with Karbhari and Pendlebury (1997), where the question of whether the underlying belief behind the creation of agencies in the UK (that is, giving managers significant freedom to manage their agency would lead to the provision of more effective and efficient services) had been delivered by the NSI programme. The findings suggested that senior managers perceived that, as a result of the agency programme, they have more freedom and control of their activities and, perhaps more importantly, they were providing a more effective service and giving increased value for money.

In respect of the perceived drawbacks, the majority of chief executives were aware of difficulties that had arisen or could arise from an approach that emphasises mission statements, objectives, targets and performance measures. There was no impression given of insurmountable adverse consequences, but rather a sense that as problems arose they had to be managed, and as new systems were introduced they may have to be adjusted at the early stages to make them appropriate. This contrasts with the evidence provided by other researchers (such as Hopwood, 1985; Smith, 1993; Mol, 1996) who illustrate extreme difficulties of utilising a tightly coupled planning and control system and highlight the dysfunctional consequences. Perhaps the different findings in this research result from the different organisational form studied, agencies being possibly less complex and more focused than many other public-sector organisations. Conceivably, the degree of 'tightness' in the coupling of the planning and control systems of agencies is less than in other organisations (as discussed previously), and this may reduce potential dysfunctional consequences. With regard to agencies, no evidence was found to support the suggestion by Sharifi and Bovaird (1995) that the use of a more rational approach had led to a 'lip-service' or ritualistic response by organisations. This suggestion was largely dismissed by chief executives and considerable 'commitment to the cause' was demonstrated (although it should be noted that there is no evidence here that all managers in agencies have similar perceptions). The degree of flexibility with which systems were developed and operated in Northern Ireland agencies may have been a contributing factor to this response. Moreover, the relatively small size of the Northern Ireland agencies compared with the British agencies might result in fewer difficulties.

It is interesting to note that, with reference to the degree of completeness of the linkages between objectives, targets and performance measures, the perceptions of chief executives were generally of fairly complete systems, whereas the empirical evidence reported in Chapters 5 and 6 demonstrates considerable gaps. For example, although respondents identified some difficulties in developing targets for particular objectives, these were fairly limited. Moreover, regarding the possibility of a target being developed that was unrelated to an objective, the vast majority of chief executives perceived that this would not happen because of the review process. However, little evidence was given of a deliberate attempt formally to establish or review linkages between objectives and targets, although most chief executives were of the opinion that these links were fairly strong. As seen in Chapter 5, even when work-programme targets were excluded, 23 per cent of the targets in the business plans could not be related to objectives. Furthermore, as shown in Chapter 6, over 36 per cent of the performance measures used in the annual reports were unrelated to targets in the business plans.

Although the above figures relate to all 24 agencies, and only nine chief executives of Northern Ireland agencies were interviewed, it was clear to the interviewers (because of the availability of the individual analysis and map for each agency) that the degree of linkage suggested by the chief executives' responses was often much greater than that suggested by the analysis of the individual agency documents. To ensure continued goodwill, it was decided not to confront chief executives with the analysis during the interview (such confrontation may possibly have suggested that they did not know the extent of linkages or were misrepresenting the extent).

It is possible, because of the method used and the lack of detailed knowledge of the agency by the researchers, that the extent of the linkages identified from the analysis in the previous two chapters was understated. However, this understatement is unlikely to have been severe. The fact that no deliberate attempt formally to review the links between objectives, targets and performance measures was described, led the researchers to conclude that gaps can arise without the knowledge of the senior management of agencies.

Hyndman and Anderson (1997a, 1998), although not dealing with the same issue as the linkages between objectives, targets and performance measures, identified significant gaps in the range of targets developed by agencies and a failure on the part of some agencies to report on important aspects of performance. As in this case, a lack of review may be a causal factor. Concerns relating to this are discussed in Chapters 5 and 6. For example, if an aspect of performance is being measured (and being valued) that is unrelated to a target, unrelated to an objective and unrelated to the overall mission of the agency, this may result in an inappropriate focus (and inappropriate activity) and a waste of resources. Similarly, if an objective is stated yet no targets related to that objective are developed, then it is possible, or indeed probable, that activities that support that objective will receive limited attention. These gaps can undermine an agency's attempts to both improve management and provide greater accountability. A more formal review of the mission statement, objectives, targets and performance measures within each agency, perhaps with the production of maps internally to support such a process, might avoid these potential adverse consequences.

With reference to the use of targets as the basis for accountability, the interviews provided some explanation regarding the findings in Chapter 6, where it was discovered that the vast majority of performance measures that were related to targets were related to key targets. Most of the respondents highlighted that key targets were largely used for external reporting, with other (non-key) targets being used primarily for internal purposes. This would accord with HM Treasury (1992) guidance, be fairly logical in that key targets tend to be high level and cover critical success areas, and possibly avoid the potential danger of information overload. This accountability was seen by many of the chief executives as equally important to the objective of improving management as it gave a visibility to what was going on.

In terms of the various stakeholders (for example, customers, the agency and the parent department), chief executives were of the view that, whereas customers tended to view quality targets as most important, the parent department was most concerned with financial targets. This confirms a similar finding by Karbhari and Pendlebury (1997), when researching British agencies, that senior managers of agencies sense that financial performance is really what matters and assessments of their personal performance are significantly affected by their ability to meet such targets. Possibly this is merely confirming an overriding constraining influence of financial resources on the activities of the agency, an influence that both public- and private-sector organisations experience to varying degrees. In respect of the agencies themselves, an impression was given of chief executives taking a more holistic view and attempting to balance customers' demands with parent department needs.

Although the publication of an annual report by the agencies was accepted as part of the agency culture, and the fairly hands-on involvement of some chief executives was evidenced, a few respondents questioned whether there was much interest in such documents. It was stated that few members of the public requested the annual report. However, examples were given where interested parties, such as lobby groups and the media, would use such documents to publicise the performance of the agency (perhaps, in the opinion of the chief executive, in a skewed or unfair manner).

Without entering the debate regarding the distinction between 'interest of the public', possibly as evidenced by avid readership of annual reports, and 'public interest', possibly facilitated by transparency and possible scrutiny by a few interested parties, it is clear that the publication of annual reports was viewed by chief executives as an important matter. As discussed in Chapter 3, it has been argued that whereas a lack of disclosure may suit some managers, the external pressure provided by the publication of information encourages a focus for the organisation and provides a catalyst for managers as they seek to improve performance. Similarly, it is suggested that the absence of accountability makes inappropriate actions by an organisation much more likely. Given these concerns, and acknowledging the need to consider cost–benefit issues, there would seem to be a *prima facie* case for reporting through such a medium.

The research included in this chapter complements the research presented in the previous two chapters and, indeed, other recent studies of the agency sector. It focuses on the perceptions of chief executives in agencies operating in Northern Ireland. As such, it is a case study within the wider UK agency sector and therefore any generalising of the conclusions beyond the Northern Ireland context should be undertaken with care. However, although the average size of Northern Ireland agencies is relatively small compared with British agencies, there are significant similarities between the modes of operation of all agencies in the UK. Furthermore, a number of the agencies in Northern Ireland have directly comparable agencies operating in Great Britain, albeit on a larger scale. Moreover, the issues of targeting and quantification are common to all agencies, as is the guidance provided to support such activities.

8

Conclusions

This chapter reviews the objectives of the research and some of the key themes with regard to rational management and accountability. Although detailed conclusions regarding the empirical studies are presented at the end of Chapters 5–7, a summary of the main findings is provided. Finally, suggestions for further research are made.

8.1 Objectives of the report

The agency sector grew out of the Efficiency Unit's report *Improving Management in Government: The Next Steps* (Efficiency Unit, 1988) that argued that the civil service was too large and diverse to manage as a single entity and that there was a need for smaller, performance-focused units. The Government promptly accepted the main recommendations of the report and inaugurated the continuing process, referred to as the NSI, of establishing agencies. A key aspect of this was the articulation and application of a more rational approach to management with its emphasis on quantification.

The main objective of the NSI is to bring about better performance in the delivery of central-government services, and, as a result of the NSI, the importance of targeting, measuring and reporting performance increased. This was seen in the emphasis placed by the Treasury on the development of co-ordinated objectives and targets in the planning documents of agencies and the heightened importance given to the inclusion of performance information in their annual reports. It was argued that this would give focus to their activities, provide a basis for evaluating performance and aid the discharge of accountability.

The main objectives of this research report were:

- To review the rationale and difficulties of using a highly rational model of management in the public sector, with its focus on targeting, measuring and reporting performance. This includes an analysis of the movement from a concentration on administration to the adoption of new-style management processes under NPM. A particular emphasis is placed on the need to co-ordinate the mission statements, objectives and targets within planning documents, and for these to be consistent with the performance measures used in external reports.
- To identify the degree to which the mission statement, objectives and targets in the corporate and business plans of agencies are consistent, complete and co-ordinated, and the extent to which these are used to provide a basis for external reporting (via the medium of the annual report).

- To identify the perceptions of chief executives of agencies in Northern Ireland in respect of the development, use and impact of mission statements, objectives, targets and performance measures. This aspect of the research represents a case study within the wider UK agency sector.

8.2 Rational management and accountability

In recent years the emphasis in public-sector management has moved from administration to rational management (which stresses, among other things, quantification). One aspect of this focus on rational management was the creation of agencies. Significant themes connected to rational management are that strategy should come about by highly systematised forms of planning and that there is a need for specific and quantified targets. Ideas from the rational management literature, similar to those found in the writings of Drucker and Argenti, proliferate in many of the UK government publications related to planning and control in the public sector. Such an approach is concerned with defining the problem, developing alternative solutions, placing values on the consequences of various alternatives, assessing the probability that they will occur, and making a decision based on logical rules (Chandler and Plano, 1988). Themes often associated with such an approach are a top-down focus with senior management of the organisation determining and directing strategy, the development of a strategy for the organisation as a whole prior to the construction of supporting strategies for individual business units or functions, and individual strategies being evaluated objectively.

In relation to this scheme, a number of writers have stressed the importance of the linkages between the various levels of planning and control. For example, Meekings (1995) argues that a well-co-ordinated set of targets and performance measures can support management, and suggests a performance-measurement framework consisting of a top-to-bottom measurement architecture, a systematic review architecture, and an integrated planning and budgeting process. Although many government publications have stressed such ideas, the rational approach faces many criticisms. These include the inability of management (in terms of analytical skills and time) to operate such a model, the tendency to overemphasise quantitative performance measures and disregard the qualitative and strategic elements in decision making, and the tendency to ignore the political and cultural contexts in which decision making takes place.

Alternative models of management in the public sector are the incremental model and the logical incremental model. Taken together, these three models do not define precisely how planning takes place in organisations, but rather represent typical tendencies in planning. The incremental model is most associated with Lindblom (1959). It stresses the decision-making sequence as follows: identify the problem; investigate how similar problems have been handled in the past; analyse and evaluate a few solutions that appear to be plausible; and choose one that makes some contribution to solving the problem without drastically altering existing processes and institutions (Chandler and Plano, 1988). However, the incremental model also faces sharp criticisms. These include an inability (because of its inbuilt conservative bias) to promote appropriate change where radical new approaches are needed, and its tendency to accept existing methods, structures and processes.

The logical incremental model can be viewed as a 'middle way'. With it, strategy emerges through a constant process of analysis, reanalysis and modification throughout the development and implementation of strategy in order to keep in line with the environment. The main difference between incrementalism and logical incrementalism is the sense of logic and rationality in the latter. However, logical incrementalism, unlike rational management, should not be seen in terms of a neat sequential model. The idea that strategy is the end result of a rational analysis of all possible options does not hold.

Accountability can be viewed as the requirement to explain or justify what has been done, what is being done, and what has been planned. The linkages between the planning system and the discharge of accountability are clear. A rational management approach stresses the importance of objectives and targets in supporting management as they plan and control the operation of an organisation. However, such objectives and targets could also provide the basis for the discharge of performance accountability.

8.3 The empirical studies

Empirical studies of 24 matched sets of documents (business plan, corporate plan and annual report) were undertaken to ascertain the degree to which the mission statements, objectives and targets in the corporate and business plans of agencies are consistent, complete and co-ordinated. The extent to which these are used to provide a basis for external reporting (via the medium of the annual report) was also investigated. In addition, a series of interviews with chief executives of agencies in Northern Ireland was undertaken, focusing on the development, use and impact of mission statements, objectives, targets and performance measures. This aspect represented a case study within the wider UK agency sector, and therefore caution needs to be exercised in 'reading across' the findings to British agencies. However, all UK agencies have very similar modes of operation and corresponding concentrations on the importance of targeting and measuring performance. The main findings of the research are as follow.

8.3.1 The evidence of a rigid rational model is weak

It is argued that if a highly rational management approach is being used, then objectives would be clearly linked to a mission statement, each objective would have a number of key targets, and each key target would spawn a number of linked operational targets. Furthermore, all objectives would have targets, and no targets would be unrelated to objectives. The empirical studies show that this is not the case in the agency sector. For example, using the method outlined in this report, approximately 44 per cent of the objectives in the corporate plans had no related targets, and 23 per cent of the targets (excluding work-programme targets) in the business plans could not be related to objectives. It is suggested that this lack of linkage indicates a possible weakness. For example, if targets are set for activities that are unrelated to objectives, then it is likely that these activities will be emphasised and supported whether or not they further the overall mission of the agency. The evidence from the interviews also suggested something less inflexible than the rational management model as normally described. For example, a sequential process commencing with the formulation of a mission statement and then proceeding to objectives and targets is typically presented. However, in the vast majority of agencies, the sequencing was not rigid and in most cases the chief executive described the process as being iterative.

8.3.2 Chief executives are unaware of the lack of linkages

Although the chief executives acknowledged that at times it was difficult to develop targets for all objectives, the degree of linkage suggested by them was much stronger than that indicated by the analysis of business and corporate plans. The fact that no deliberate attempt formally to review the links between objectives, targets and performance measures was described led the researchers to conclude that gaps can arise without the knowledge of the senior management of agencies. This gives rise to a number of concerns similar to those mentioned above. For example, if an objective is stated yet no targets related to that objective are developed, then it is possible, or indeed probable, that activities that support that objective will receive limited attention. These gaps may undermine an agency's attempts to both improve management and provide greater accountability. It is possible that a more formal review of the mission statement, objectives, targets and performance measures within each agency, perhaps with the production of maps internally to support such a process, might avoid these potential adverse consequences.

8.3.3 Relatively, the degree of linkage is greater than in other related studies

The extent of the weaknesses identified above should not be exaggerated. When compared with previous studies in other sectors, the results in this study show much greater degrees of linkage. For example, excluding work-programme targets, over 80 per cent of targets could be related to objectives. Such a figure is extremely high when compared with the findings of Brace et al. (1980) and Thompson (1995). This, taken with the maps of individual agencies, many of which show reasonably tightly coupled sets of mission statements, objectives, targets and performance measures, provides evidence of a significantly greater degree of linkage than is found elsewhere. Indeed, this finding is perhaps of great encouragement to those who advocate the applicability of models of management based on quantification in the agency sector. Given that other studies of the agency sector have suggested that improvements in performance-measurement systems have occurred over time (Hyndman and Anderson, 1998), the relatively high degree of co-ordination presently displayed by agencies may be capable of even further enhancement.

8.3.4 *Evidence of flexibility in the systems*

A more flexible approach to the concept of rational management than that which is implied by a rigid rational management model is suggested by Tomkins (1987). Although acknowledging the imperfections of a totally comprehensive rational management model, he argues that it is the only model that has a general logic and acceptability to those charged with making progress in the public sector. He highlights the need for rational analysis (that is, the process of identifying cause and effect) where possible, rather than totally rationalistic systems. It could be that, although often articulated in rational management terminology, planning and control systems in the public sector are much more flexible in practical application and are more akin to the logical incremental model (Quinn, 1980). This research provides support for the possibility of this more flexible approach. For example, it could be that, because of the difficulties of identifying cause-and-effect relationships in some agencies, specific targets related to certain objectives are viewed as unhelpful, and judgement is used to interpret results. Moreover, the interviews with chief executives, although providing evidence that financial controls are tight, abound with examples of the manner in which mission statements, objectives and targets are developed, and feedback information used, that demonstrate considerable flexibility.

8.3.5 *Chief executives perceive major benefits from the use of more rational systems, and limited drawbacks*

The chief executives perceived that the importance of rational analysis and performance reporting had increased since agencification and that, overall, this had brought significant benefits. By far the most frequently quoted was the sense of increased focus that it facilitated. Furthermore, all the chief executives believed that this had resulted in benefits to the agency itself, the parent department and the customer. These findings are in line with Karbhari and Pendlebury (1997). Regarding perceived drawbacks, most chief executives were aware of difficulties that had arisen or could arise from an approach that emphasises mission statements, objectives, targets and performance measures. However, there was no impression given of insurmountable adverse consequences, but rather a sense that as problems arose they could be managed.

8.3.6 *The key targets in the planning documents provide a basis for the reporting of performance*

The empirical studies provide evidence that the targets contained in the planning documents lay down a basis for the reporting of performance through the mechanism of the annual report. Although there are far fewer performance measures in the annual reports than targets in the planning documents, the majority of performance measures are related to targets in the business plans (approximately 64 per cent). Furthermore, it is also clear that it is the key targets of agencies that form the platform for reporting. Over 84 per cent of key targets in the business plans had at least one related performance measure in the annual reports. The interviews with chief executives highlighted an awareness of the importance of key targets in external reporting.

The process of discharging accountability gives a visibility to the resources, activities and achievements of an organisation, thus enabling informed discussions and decisions by users. This need to report against key targets encourages management to focus on the issues that are of importance to those stakeholders who are outside the immediate management of the organisation.

8.4 Further research

The research included in this report complements other recent studies of the agency sector. However, further research is needed to understand better the impact that rational analysis and performance reporting has had and can have on the management of, and external reporting by, agencies. There are a number of other potential research areas that could be explored relating to this work. Surveys of the views of the managers of parent departments, managers within the agency (other than chief executives), users of the service and other stakeholders could be undertaken. These may give a richer understanding of the changes that have taken place and help to ascertain the appropriateness of the objectives, targets and performance measures used. Moreover, this may allow the identification of the extent of the ownership of targets by managers at various levels in the agency, a condition that is often viewed as a necessary prerequisite for performance improvement. The importance of the recognition of context in the operation of planning and control systems has been highlighted in this report. A disaggregation of the data into areas of service activity within the wider agency sector may provide a better understanding of this and encourage the development of more appropriate, customised systems. Studies of the possible impact of alternative financing arrangements on the management and reporting systems of agencies could also provide insights. The issues investigated in this research report and many of the other potential research areas have relevance to other public-sector organisations and the wider NFPO sector. Studies (possibly of a comparative nature) in other parts of the UK public sector, in the public sectors of other countries (especially those that have embraced NPM), or in other NFPOs would aid understanding.

Appendix

Interview guide

Question	
1.	How long have you worked in the agency (or function)?
2.	Are you broadly aware of the terms 'mission', 'objective', 'target' and 'performance measure'?
3.	What is the difference between 'key targets' and 'other (non-key) targets'?
4.	To what extent have you been directly or indirectly involved in the development of mission statements, objectives, targets and performance measures in the agency? How would you describe your involvement? • Very involved • Quite involved • Reasonably involved • A little involved • Not involved at all
5.	To what extent (or 'to what extent do you believe' if the individual had not worked in the organisation prior to agencification) has the importance of mission statements, objectives, targets and performance measures changed since agencification?
6.	How was the mission statement developed?
7.	In what order were the mission statement, objectives and targets developed?
8.	Is it possible/likely that an objective would be established and no targets developed relating to this objective? Is there a deliberate attempt to ensure that there are targets for each objective? What form does this take?
9.	Is it possible/likely that a target would be established unrelated to an objective? If so, why?
10.	Are there important areas of performance of the agency that are not capable of being captured within objectives and targets, and measured through quantitative performance measures related to targets? If so, what?
11.	Have the targets that are developed been stretching (that is, as far as possible is an attempt made to improve on previous levels of performance)? Is there any evidence of this in the agency? Is any attempt made to set an easy target so that achievement can be ensured?
12.	Are the targets used routinely in reporting back to management on actual performance? Frequency, manner, reasons?
13.	Are the targets used routinely in reporting back to the sponsoring department (or minister) on actual performance? Frequency, manner, reasons?
14.	If targets are missed, what are the consequences: • Within the agency? • From the perspective of the sponsoring department (or minister)?

Question	
15.	From an agency management perspective, which of the following types of targets are seen as most important? • Financial targets (for example, live within budget, sales revenue generated) • Volume (for example, number of cases handled) • Efficiency (for example, cost per vehicle tested, cases handled per employee) • Quality (for example, waiting time, error rate) Same question to be asked from: • A sponsoring department perspective, and • The public's or customers' perspective.
16.	Are targets used in discharging a wider external accountability, possibly through the mechanism of the annual report?
17.	What are the benefits of a management approach that emphasises mission statements, objectives, targets and performance measures?
18.	In terms of the use of targets, is the most important objective: • The improvement of management? or is it • Greater accountability?
19.	Overall, do you believe that a focus on mission, objectives, targets and performance measures has improved the performance of the agency? From whose point of view? Can you give me any evidence of this?
20.	What are the drawbacks of a management approach that emphasises mission, objectives, targets and performance measures?
21.	To what extent could the pursuit of targets lead to inappropriate decisions or behaviour in the agency? Could you give an example(s)?
22.	To what extent has the organisation's focusing on mission statements, objectives, targets and performance measures been 'ritualistic', with little real commitment to the cause (that is, paying 'lip-service' to the need to develop such systems without any real desire to see change)?

Notes

1 Hood (1991) suggested that NPM is a convenient, though rather loose, term that is shorthand for a set of broadly similar administrative doctrines that dominated the reform agenda in the public sector in many OECD countries from the late 1970s. Moreover, he identifies the main themes of NPM as being 'the idea of a shift in emphasis from policy making to management skills, from a stress on process to a stress on output, from orderly hierarchies to an intendedly more competitive basis for providing public services, from fixed to variable pay and from a uniform and inclusive public service to a variant structure with more emphasis on contract provision' (Hood, 1995, p. 95).

2 To facilitate the development of the research to ascertain the extent to which the targets are used to provide a basis for external reporting (via the medium of the annual report), business plans and corporate plans were analysed which contained objectives and targets for periods that related to years for which annual reports were later made available. For example, the corporate plan 1994–7 and the business plan 1996/97 would be used with the annual report 1996/97. This would enable the investigation of the use of performance information in the annual reports of agencies and to relate this to the mission statement, objectives, key targets and other (non-key) targets included in the planning documents in a meaningful manner.

3 To avoid major difficulties of analysis, agencies were excluded if they had over 200 targets. This rule led to one agency being excluded.

4 In one case the acting chief executive was interviewed. In another case the deputy chief executive was interviewed because of the unavailability of the chief executive.

5 This statement is speculative, based on intuition. This issue could be tested by further research that hypothesises different degrees of linkage between agencies that provide 'routine' and 'non-routine' tasks. No attempt is made to do this in this research report.

6 Some writers, mainly from the critical accounting school, have questioned the all-pervasive influence of rational management (and resulting 'accountingisation') on the public sector (see Power and Laughlin, 1992; Chua and Preston, 1994). It is not our intention to explore the merits of these arguments.

7 In a number of cases one performance measurement covered more than one target. For example, the Public Trust Office had three separate targets related to caseload: lodgements caseload, suitors caseload and casework caseload. However, one performance measure of total caseload was given in the annual report. Therefore each target had one related performance measure (albeit not an exact expression of the measurement base used in drafting the target), even though there was only one performance measurement overall. In a smaller number of cases one target spawned more than one performance measure. For example, the Coastguard Agency had a target to maintain a 24-hour search and rescue co-ordinating capability. In its annual report there were a number of performance measures relating to this, including the percentage of time communications equipment was available and the percentage of time coastal response vehicles were available. Therefore there were a number of performance measures relating to one target. These factors account for minor apparent inconsistencies between Table 6.3 and Tables 6.1 and 6.2, although no inconsistency actually exists.

8 A 'Fraser figure', so named after the author of the Fraser Report (HM Government, 1991), is an individual within the parent department who is a focal contact point for the agency. The role of the 'Fraser figure' is, among other things (Next Steps Team, 1995, p.7), 'to challenge the performance of the chief executive of the agency and support and facilitate the chief executive's work in relation to his/her objectives and future targets'.

References

AAA (1966), A *Statement of Basic Accounting Theory,* AAA, Sarasota.

AAA (1989), *Measuring the Performance of Non-profit Organisations: The State of the Art,* AAA, Sarasota.

ASC (1975), *The Corporate Report,* ASC, London.

Ansoff, H.I. (1979), *Strategic Management,* Macmillan, London.

Anthony, R.N. (1978), *Financial Accounting in Non-business Organisations: An Exploratory Study of Conceptual Issues,* FASB, Stamford.

Anthony, R.N. (1980), 'Making sense of nonbusiness accounting', *Harvard Business Review* (May–June), pp. 86–90.

Anthony, R.N. and Young, D.W. (1999), *Management Control in Nonprofit Organisations,* 6th edition, Irwin, Boston.

Argenti, J. (1968), *Corporate Planning: A Practical Guide,* George Allen & Unwin, Northampton.

Argenti, J. (1989), *Practical Corporate Planning,* Unwin Hyman, London.

Bailey, A. and Johnson, G. (1997), 'Logical or processural? Defining incrementalism', *Cranfield Working Paper Series,* SWP 6/97.

Birrell, W.D. (1978), 'The Northern Ireland civil service – from devolution to direct rule', *Public Administration,* 56 (2), pp. 305–20.

Boyne, G. and Law, J. (1991), 'Accountability and local authority annual reports: the case of Welsh District Councils', *Financial Accountability & Management,* 7 (4), pp. 179–94.

Brace, P., Elkin, R., Robinson, D.D. and Steinberg, H.I. (1980), *Reporting of Service Efforts and Accomplishments* (Research Report), FASB, Stamford.

Butani, K.N. (1966), 'Implementing administrative innovations and reforms', *Indian Journal of Public Administration,* 12, pp. 612–17.

Cabinet Office (2000), *How to Review Agencies and Non-departmental Public Bodies to Improve the Quality and Effectiveness of Public Services,* Cabinet Office, London.

Carter, N. (1991), 'Learning to measure performance: the use of indicators in organisations', *Public Administration,* 69, pp. 85–101.

Carter, N., Klein, K. and Day, P. (1992), *How Organisations Measure Success: The Use of Performance Indicators in Government,* Routledge, London.

Chandler, R.C. and Plano, J.C. (1988), *The Public Administration Dictionary,* ABC–CLIO, Santa Barbara.

Chua, W.F. and Preston, A. (1994), 'Worrying about accounting health care', *Accounting, Auditing & Accountability Journal,* 7 (3), pp. 4–17.

Dearlove, J. (1979), *The Reorganisation of British Local Government,* Cambridge University Press, Cambridge.

DFP (1984), *Progress in Financial Management in Northern Ireland Departments,* Stationery Office, Belfast.

Drucker, P. (1954), *The Practice of Management,* Harper & Row, New York.

Drucker, P. (1976), 'What results should you expect? A user's guide to MBO', *Public Administration Review,* 36, pp. 12–9.

Drucker, P. (1980), 'The deadly sins in public administration', *Public Administration Review,* 40, pp. 103–6.

Drucker, P. (1990), *Managing the Non-profit Organisation,* Butterworth-Heinemann, Oxford.

DuPont-Morales, M.A. and Harris, J.E. (1994), 'Strengthening accountability: incorporating strategic planning and performance measurement into budgeting', *Public Productivity and Management Review,* 17, pp. 231–9.

Earl, M.J. and Hopwood, A.G. (1980), 'From management information to information management', in H.C. Lucas et al. (eds), *The Information Systems Environment,* North-Holland, New York.

Eden, R. and Hyndman, N. (1999), 'Performance measurement in the UK public sector: poisoned chalice or Holy Grail?', *Optimum, The Journal of the Public Sector,* 29 (1), pp. 9–15.

Edwards, M. and Hulme, D. (1995), *Non-governmental Organisations – Performance and Accountability (Beyond the Magic Bullet),* Earthscan, London.

Efficiency Unit (1988), *Improving Management in Government: The Next Steps. A Report to the Prime Minister,* Stationery Office, London.

Emmanuel, C., Otley, D. and Merchant, K. (1990), *Accounting for Management Control,* 2nd edition, Chapman & Hall, London.

FASB (1980), *Statement of Financial Accounting Concepts No. 4: Objectives of Financial Reporting by Non-business Organisations,* FASB, Stamford.

Firth, D. and Leigh, A. (1998), *The Corporate Fool,* Capstone, Oxford.

Fox, J. (1992), 'Democratic rural development: leadership accountability in regional peasant organisations', *Development and Change,* 23 (2), pp. 1–36.

GASB (1987), *Concepts Statement No 1: Objectives of Financial Reporting,* GASB, Stamford.

GASB (1993), *Codification of Governmental Accounting and Financial Reporting Standards as of June 30, 1993,* GASB, Stamford.

Gibson, J.L. (1978), 'Performance indicators in the court system', in H. Greer et al. (eds), *Accountability in Urban Society,* Sage, London.

Gray, R. (1983), 'Accounting, financial reporting and not-for-profit organisations', *AUTA Review,* 15 (1), pp. 3–23.

Gray, R. (1984), 'Uncharitable view of accounting', *Accountancy,* August, p. 84.

Hansmann, H. (1996), 'The changing roles of public, private and nonprofit enterprise in education, healthcare and other human services', in V. Fuchs (ed.), *Individual and Social Responsibility: Child Care, Education, Medical Care and Long-term Care in America,* Chicago University Press, Chicago.

Hatry, H., Fountain, J., Sullivan, J. and Kremer, L. (eds) (1990), *Service Efforts and Accomplishments Reporting: Its Time Has Come* (Research Report), GASB, Stamford.

Hedlund, R.D. and K.E. Hamm (1978), 'Accountability and political institutions', in H. Greer et al. (eds), *Accountability in Urban Society,* Sage, London.

HM Government (1968), *Report of the Committee on the Civil Service* (The Fulton Report), Cmnd. 3638, Stationery Office, London.

HM Government (1982), *Efficiency and Effectiveness in the Civil Service,* Cm. 8616, Stationery Office, London.

HM Government (1990), *Improving Management in Government: The Next Steps Agencies. Review 1990,* Cm. 1261, Stationery Office, London.

HM Government (1991), *Management of Ministers' Departments and their Executive Agencies. A report to the Prime Minister (Fraser Report),* Stationery Office, London.

HM Government (1995), *Better Accounting for the Taxpayer's Money; Resource Accounting and Budgeting in Government,* Cm. 2929, Stationery Office, London.

HM Government (1996), *Next Steps Review 1995,* Cm. 3164, Stationery Office, London.

HM Government (1997), *Next Steps Review 1996,* Cm. 3579, Stationery Office, London.

HM Government (1999), *Modernising Government,* Cm. 4310, Stationery Office, London.

HM Treasury (1989), *The Financing and Accountability of Next Steps Agencies,* Cm. 914, Stationery Office, London.

HM Treasury (1992), *Executive Agencies: A Guide to Setting Targets and Measuring Performance,* Stationery Office, London.

Hood, C. (1991), 'A public management for all seasons!', *Public Administration,* 69, pp. 3–19.

Hood, C. (1995), 'The "New Public Management" in the 1980s: variations on a theme', *Accounting, Organisations and Society,* 20 (3), pp. 93–109.

Hood, C. (1996), 'Beyond "progressivism": a new "global paradigm" in public management?', *International Journal of Public Administration,* 19 (2), pp. 151–78.

Hopwood, A.G. (1985), 'Accounting and the domain of the public: some observations on current developments', *The Price Waterhouse Public Lecture on Accounting,* University of Leeds, November.

Hyndman, N. (1990), 'Charity accounting – an empirical study of the information needs of contributors to UK fund-raising charities', *Financial Accountability & Management,* 6 (4), pp. 295–307.

Hyndman, N. and Anderson, R. (1997a), 'A study of the use of quantitative targets in the planning documents of executive agencies', *Financial Accountability & Management,* 13 (2), pp. 139–64.

Hyndman, N. and Anderson, R. (1997b), *The Use of Performance Information in External Reporting and Internal Planning: A Study of Executive Agencies,* Association of Chartered Certified Accountants' Research Report (No. 52), Certified Accountants Educational Trust, London.

Hyndman, N. and Anderson, R. (1998), 'Performance information, accountability and executive agencies', *Public Money & Management,* 18 (2), pp. 23–31.

ICAS (1988), *Making Corporate Reports Valuable,* Kogan Page, London.

Johnson, G. and Scholes, K. (1999), *Exploring Corporate Strategy,* 5th edition, Prentice Hall, Hemel Hempstead.

Jones, R. and Pendlebury, M. (1996), *Public Sector Accounting,* 4th edition, Pitman, London.

Kanter, R. and Summers, D. (1987), 'Doing well while doing good: dilemmas of performance measurement in nonprofit organisations and the need for a multiple constituency approach', in W. Powell (ed.), *Handbook of Nonprofit Organisations,* Yale University Press, New Haven.

Kaplan, R.S and Norton, D.P. (1996), T*he Balanced Scorecard: Translating Strategy into Action,* Harvard Business School Press, Boston.

Karbhari, Y. and Pendlebury, M. (1997), *The Impact of the Executive Agencies Programme on Accounting, Accountability and Effectiveness,* Association of Chartered Certified Accountants' Research Report (No. 53), Certified Accountants Educational Trust, London.

Knox, C. and McHugh, M. (1990), 'Management in government – the "Next Steps" in Northern Ireland', *Administration,* 38 (3), pp. 251–70.

Lapsley, I. (1998), 'Reforming the public sector: demon accountants at work??', *Irish Accounting Review,* 5 (1), pp. 115–31.

Likierman, A. (1993), 'Performance indicators: 20 early lessons from managerial use', *Public Money & Management,* 13 (4), pp. 15-22.

Likierman, A. (1997), 'Applying accruals-based accounting and budgeting to UK central government', *Irish Accounting Review,* 4 (2), pp. 55–68.

Likierman, A. and Creasey, P. (1985), 'Objectives and entitlement to rights in government financial information', *Financial Accountability & Management,* 1 (1), pp. 33–50.

Lindblom, C.E. (1959), 'The science of muddling through', *Public Administration Review,* 9, pp. 70–88.

Lindblom, C.E. (1965), *The Intelligence of Democracy,* Free Press, New York.

Loughlin, J. (1992), 'Administering policy in Northern Ireland', in B. Hadfield (ed.), *Northern Ireland Politics and the Constitution,* Open University Press, Buckingham.

Mayston, D. (1985), 'Non-profit performance indicators in the public sector', *Financial Accountability & Management,* 1 (1), pp. 51–74.

Mayston, D. (1992), 'Capital accounting, user needs and the foundations of a conceptual framework for public-sector financial reporting', *Financial Accountability & Management,* 8 (4), pp. 227–48.

McSweeney, B. (1988), 'Accounting for the audit commission', *Political Quarterly,* 59, pp. 28–43.

Meekings, A. (1995), 'Unlocking the potential of performance measurement: a practical implementation guide', *Public Money & Management,* 15 (4), pp. 5–12.

Mol, P.N. (1996), 'Performance indicators in the Dutch department of defence', *Financial Accountability & Management,* 12 (1), pp. 71–81.

Next Steps Briefing Note (1996) April, Office of Public Service, London.

Next Steps Team, Office of Public Service (1995), *The Strategic Management of Agencies,* Stationery Office, London.

Ouchi, W.G. (1979), 'A conceptual framework for the design of organisational control models', *Management Science*, 25, pp. 833–48.

Pendlebury, M., Jones, R. and Karbhari, Y. (1994), 'Developments in the accountability and financial reporting practices of executive agencies', *Financial Accountability & Management*, 10 (1), pp. 33–46.

Phyrr, P.A. (1973), *Zero Base Budgeting*, John Wiley, New York.

Power, M. and Laughlin, R. (1992), 'Critical theory and accounting', in M. Alvesson and H. Wilmott (eds), *Critical Management Studies*, Sage, London.

Public Accounts Committee (1997), *Resource Accounting and Proposals for a Resource-based System of Supply, Committee of Public Accounts, 9th Report, Session 1996–97,* HC 167 , Stationery Office, London.

Quinn, J.B. (1980), *Strategies for Change, Logical Incrementalism*, Irwin, Homewood.

Quinn, J.B. (1982), 'Managing strategy incrementally', *OMEGA – International Journal of Management Science*, 10 (6), pp. 613–27.

Rutherford, B.A. (1983), *Financial Reporting in the Public Sector*, Butterworths, London.

Schilit, W.K. and Paine, F.T. (1987), 'An examination of the underlying dynamics of strategic decisions subject to upward influence activity', *Journal of Management Studies*, 24 (2), pp.161–87.

Sharifi, S. and Bovaird, T. (1995), 'The financial management initiative in the UK public sector: the symbolic role of performance reporting', *International Journal of Public Administration*, 18 (2/3), pp. 467–90.

Simon, H.A. (1976), *Administrative Behaviour: A Study of Decision-making Processes in Administration*, 3rd edition, Free Press, New York.

Smith, P. (1993), 'Outcome-related performance indicators and organisational control in the public sector', *British Journal of Management*, 4, pp. 135–51.

Stewart, J. (1984), 'The role of information in public accountability', in A.G. Hopwood and C.R. Tomkins (eds), *Issues in Public Sector Accounting*, Philip Allan, Oxford.

Stewart, J. and Walsh, K. (1994), 'Performance measurement: when performance can never be finally defined', *Public Money & Management*, 14 (2), pp. 45–9.

Stonich, P.J. (1977), *Zero Base Budgeting – Improved Cost Control and Resource Allocation*, Dow Jones–Irwin, New York.

Thompson, G.D. (1995), 'Problems with service performance reporting: the case of public art galleries', *Financial Accountability & Management*, 11 (4), pp. 337–55.

Tomkins, C.R. (1987), *Achieving Economy, Efficiency and Effectiveness in the Public Sector*, Kogan Page, London.

Vinzant, D.H. (1996), 'Strategic management and public organisations: lessons from the past and prescriptions for the future', *International Journal of Public Administration*, 19, pp. 1743–79.

Wildavsky, A. (1964), *The Politics of the Budgetary Process*, Little Brown, Boston.